Wealth Odyssey

Wealth Odyssey

The Essential Road Map For Your Financial Journey
Where Is It You Are Really Trying To Go With Money?

Larry R. Frank Sr., MBA, CFP®
Developmental Editor: Peter Sander
Copy Editor: Maxwell Limanowski

iUniverse, Inc.
New York Lincoln Shanghai

Wealth Odyssey
The Essential Road Map For Your Financial Journey
Where Is It You Are Really Trying To Go With Money?

Copyright © 2005 by Larry R. Frank Sr.

iUniverse books may be ordered through booksellers or by contacting:

iUniverse
2021 Pine Lake Road, Suite 100
Lincoln, NE 68512
www.iuniverse.com
1-800-Authors (1-800-288-4677)

ISBN: 0-595-33720-1

Printed in the United States of America

Dedicated to my son Larry R Frank Jr.
and my wife Rosa Maria Cáceres de Frank.

Contents

Part III: Your Journey Begins

Scenic Side Trips (SSTs) Index

List of Figures

Preface

My interest is in the future because I am going to spend the rest of my life there.

—Charles F. Kettering

This book was written in response to observations made over my past decade of teaching personal finance. The 12-hour adult education course I teach covers the broad spectrum of personal finance topics. While taking the course, the adult students would often ask me, "Is there anything I could read that would give a broad perspective of what I should be doing with my money? How does each of the financial topics I've learned about fit together?" Many clients in my financial planning practice have asked the same questions. Clearly, these smart folks were looking for the picture on the box top showing what the financial puzzle would look like once they put together all their confusing financial pieces.

I have not seen such a work, so I wrote this book in response.

People have many financial concerns. They try to do—or address—everything with their money. Many feel they are putting in a lot of effort but still are not accomplishing anything. They feel lost and do not know what to focus on first. They feel lost when they try to address each of their many financial issues and concerns without looking at their overall situation. How much of what kind of insurance do I need? How much do I need to save for retirement? How should I invest? Do I need an estate plan? The list goes on.

They feel lost when they get what seems to be conflicting information about each of these topics. This is not because people do not know what to do. It is because they do not know how to address multiple issues simultaneously. How can people succeed if they have not been taught how to address things simultaneously? The financial industry has not been helpful to date, mainly because of the tendency to focus on financial *products—insurance products, investment products, and so forth*—which naturally leads to addressing one issue at a time. In *Wealth Odyssey* I offer an approach to understanding comprehensive financial planning, a box top map to help put your financial box top picture together in your mind before getting started with the pieces.

As a Certified Financial Planner™ practitioner (CFP®), I have grown accustomed to addressing multiple topics and planning for multiple goals simultaneously by showing people how their financial issues flow together. It is a matter of prioritizing and actually putting money aside for their priorities. However, it is also important to understand the big-picture ramifications of today's decisions on their future. I bring years of my own research and experience to bear since receiving a Master of Business Administration (MBA) degree in 1983 and starting my financial planning practice in 1994. Many years of rich experience in dealing with clients has shown me how money really works in people's lives. That, combined with continued research into new tools and techniques, has produced what I will share with you through this work.

The experiences I had in the military as a pilot, and later as a contingency planner, gave me insights that apply usefully in finance as well. I learned, as a pilot, to focus on getting to the destination and to consider alternatives, even before takeoff, should en-route or destination weather turn bad along the way. I also learned what set of gauges to concentrate on, depending on what it was I was doing at the time. As a contingency planner, I learned to plan with the primary objective in mind, but also to consider alternatives should something not work according to plan. All of this carries over to working with people and the development of the ideas behind this work. The ability to step back and get a lay of the land and see the *big picture*, to recognize the problem, to map out courses of action, to consider alternatives, to know what to pay attention to and when, and to adjust course as things occur—this is what I have learned in my experiences and what I will share with you.

This work is my summary of the main ideas and philosophy developed as a result of my research and reading during and beyond my MBA program, CFP® coursework and certification exam. It is my contribution to an emerging financial planning philosophy that describes financial planning as a process rather than a collection of separate products or issues. My objective is to take the results of the research currently available and to develop a practical treatment to assist real people to solve real issues in real life.

Many of the books that have served me well I have listed in Appendix E. I share that list with you so you too can have a good start with additional reading sources to help develop your wealth-building philosophy. These books also are important sources for this book. Rather than reference these source books repeatedly throughout the text, I will simply refer you to the Appendix. Through your own reading of these resources, you will develop some of your own thoughts and opinions to add to those presented here. Altogether, my purpose in writing

Wealth Odyssey and adding these resources is to point you in the right direction so you can begin your financial journey on a sound footing. Appendix F is a consolidated list so you have, at your fingertips in one easy-to-find location, various research articles that address retirement issues and sustainable withdrawal rates from portfolios. These articles form the basis for the unique philosophy I have developed and present to you in this work. The convention that I have chosen in presenting supporting material is to present it in the form of appendices so that you can concentrate on the message while reading the text and later find supporting materials when you want them. This is different from the usual method of placing the reference to supporting material as a footnote to the text. Personally, I find this method slightly distracting and hard to find when I want to go back to research a point further. Therefore, I have chosen another method that I feel will support your learning and continued research better.

This book is about the bigger picture and philosophy of wealth. It is about wealth accumulation. It is about how the topic of wealth relates to your everyday life. I base this work largely on actual financial planning experience with real people just like you. Unlike most other personal finance books, this book is *not* about:

1) tools or financial products
2) financial recipes or difficult formulas
3) getting rich quick.

As you read on, you will quickly see the difference.

This work is timeless. For you to learn more about wealth, it does not matter how much money you have right now. It does not matter where the economic cycle or market cycle is now for these principles to apply. This work simplifies complex research into an application that anyone can use to map a personal financial journey and measure their progress on that journey.

Uncommonly, I address many common misperceptions about personal finances that do little to help people actually reach solutions—for example, the perception that people will be in a lower tax bracket when they retire; the belief that simply putting money into a retirement plan, even to the maximum, is sufficient to retire with; or that individuals can somehow avoid the impact of the economy and markets by not participating in them. Read on in this work to see the many challenges these perceptions present should you fall into them.

My unique approach takes you into a different perspective about how to succeed financially and how to measure that success. I aim to change your financial lens from income and budgeting to the critical vista of net worth, better described as wealth. Net worth, not income, is a more important measure of successfully making the financial journey because it is a true measure of wealth. I developed a rare map that people can use to visualize where each financial topic falls in general and how each topic affects their financial journey. Wealth is in the center of the Wealth Odyssey Road Map (WORM) because all financial issues really center on wealth. The WORM moves income and the budget aside to change the perspective from income-based measures to wealth-based measures. To aid you in further comprehending this viewpoint, I have developed a reference point that transitions you from income-based decisions and I call this your Standard of Individual Living (SOIL). SOIL is a new and simple way to tell you where you are today. You cannot get to where you want to go without knowing where you are. To complete the transition of your perspective to a wealth-based one, the Wealth Rule is a new method to determine what level of wealth (net worth) you need in order to reach your financial destination called retirement. The Wealth Rule comes from current and ongoing research on how long money can last during withdrawals (see Appendix F). I developed the Wealth Rule to simplify the application of that research in such a way that anybody can apply it in his or her everyday life. In addition, what is also new here is a method you can *use effortlessly to determine how you are really doing* at any given time on your financial journey.

I will discuss all of these concepts throughout this work to help you learn how to use them in your life. I also weave together key financial topics so that you can see how they actually fit together on this true map of finances. Yes, someone has discussed all of these terms before and even offered solutions elsewhere, but your finances have never been described to you with *one unifying perspective* in mind, nor in such a manner that you can *easily visualize* what is important to you and measure your financial success in a simple and truly practical way. Other works have used old terminology with old perspectives to try to give you new tips. They often have concentrated on just one area of the financial map, thus missing how you can apply other important areas in their method. I know, I have read many works like that. This is a main reason I write here: to bring new meaning to old terminology so it is useful to you; to change your perspective from *income-based* to *asset-based*, which is a more meaningful measure in the 21st Century; and to help you succeed on your journey with an up-to-date application of these concepts using an updated and modern financial map.

By the time you have finished this work, you will better understand what wealth is, how to measure your wealth and how to apply that knowledge to answer some of the most perplexing financial questions you have today.

Acknowledgments

The meaning of life? To improve the lives of those around you.

I would like to acknowledge Peter Sander as an author whose insight and experience were immeasurable in getting this book written. I had this basic idea about what people were missing when they looked at their financial situation. The idea started from my perspective as a Certified Financial Planner™ (*) practitioner. Peter's challenge to me was to transform an often overlooked concept like net worth into the book before you today. (* Certified Financial Planner™, and CFP® are certification marks owned by the Certified Financial Planner Board of Standards, Inc.)

I should acknowledge important people who have contributed to my thought process throughout my life to date. They begin with Father Michael Dillon and the Rev. Herbert Franz. Both instilled in me the belief in doing the right things for the right reasons. Lloyd Dessaint once told me *luck* is labor under correct knowledge (l.u.c.k.), which has always inspired me to study and focus my energy smartly. Early on in my career in the Air Force, I was fortunate to have broadminded commanders. Lt. Col. Marc Rinehart and Col. John Bridges, both majors at that time, taught me about officership: how leaders encourage others to participate, and how each individual contributes to overall success for many. Finally, those who have influenced my thinking in my second career in the financial services industry were Gerry Reponen and Jack Root. Both illuminated my path during critical developmental periods in the early days of this second career. There are those who helped considerably to edit the manuscript and provide invaluable suggestions. For this help, I wish to thank Mark Hardy, Bernadette and Andrew Smith.

These are the opinions of the author and they do not reflect those of the Registered Investment Advisor firm I affiliate with, nor the Broker Dealer firm used to ensure I comply with securities laws, nor those of any regulatory agency or organization. Past performance does not guarantee future performance. What does this mean? It means just because something happened in the past does not mean it will happen that way again in the future.

Last but certainly not least, I acknowledge all those in my family whom I dearly love. They have taught me what life is all about. This is especially true of Conrad, Joseph, Alicia, and Larry.

Introduction

You have the right idea. You need to save. The authors of *Economics Explained* say, "In micro-economic theory, individuals get wealthy by saving, not consuming, and by earning market rates of interest upon those savings." *Affluenza. The All-Consuming Epidemic* book addresses the over-consumption problem faced by people today. The issue is really how wealth *protection* and wealth *accumulation* are related. For example, how does your 401k (or other retirement plan) relate to your life insurance? You will read later that retirement plans are one of the *Financial Tools* in the Net Worth section of the Wealth Odyssey Road Map. Life insurance also lies in this section in a supporting role. Insurance protects or replaces assets, the assets being lost income that you cannot contribute to your retirement plan due to premature death. These lost contributions are still needed for your surviving spouse's retirement, and for your family's continued living expenses. Therefore, life insurance creates an asset for you, which you *do not* currently have, to meet financial obligations you *do* currently have. Once you accumulate the asset—or once the financial obligation goes away—you do not need the insurance. Yet most people view these topics separately. This is one example of what I have seen consistently in my financial practice and teaching experience. You will see later how assets and risk management relate to each other, and how that relationship changes over your lifetime.

What are you trying to achieve by investing? How do your different financial concerns relate to each other? How do you know your progress towards meeting your different goals? What is the purpose of it all? How do you anchor yourself with an overall philosophy about what you are trying to accomplish so that you do not change everything each time you talk to someone new?

I have noticed many things while talking with people during those hundreds of class sessions. They are not saving enough for reserves, so they add every bump in life to a credit card. People are not saving enough for retirement, so they will have to work longer than they realize. People have not considered what happens if they are not able to work longer due to ill health. People are underinsured. People do not have wills and so their estate plan defaults to state law. People do not save ahead for vacation. Nor do they save enough to help with education even when

1

these are concerns they have. This list could go on. Why so many deficiencies? Observing people tells me that the focus is too much on spending money today without realizing how it affects tomorrow.

One individual came to my office with $48,000 in a retirement plan, ready to retire, he thought. He had a hopeful look on his face and a vacation travel brochure in his pocket. He had never thought about what kind of money he would need once he stopped working; he was just tired and wanted to quit. A look of sadness gradually came over him as I ran the numbers, showing that he had enough for two or three years max, *sans* vacation. Where had he gone wrong? Too little money? Too much standard of living? Both? Experience has shown repeatedly that once people understand how their short- and long-term finances fit together, they make smarter and more informed decisions as they set priorities for their money.

The Forest and the Trees

My goal is to help you realize where to place your attention. You should place it on *where* you are trying to go financially, before focusing on *how* to get there. Too many people today focus exclusively on *how* to get there. They do not have any idea where *there* is! They spend too much time on investing and have no idea for what they are investing. A vague idea is not enough. When storms arrive in the form of an unfriendly market (in *any* market—stock, bond, real estate, commodity, etc.), people become easily lost and disoriented. They are no longer sure what to do. Confusion sets in because their focus has been in the wrong place to begin with. The basic question: Are you trying to earn, through your wage or salary, a short-term income, or are you trying to grow and protect long-term wealth? The answer is long-term wealth, obviating the need for wage or salary income down the road. At the risk of oversimplifying, people become so focused on detail that they cannot see the forest for the trees. What are their concerns and goals, and what are the priorities among those concerns and goals? People are inundated with the minutiae of investing information and daily tactics. They question what is happening right now and what should one do in response to it. What is the overall strategy? More importantly, what philosophy guides their strategy and tactics regardless of minute-by-minute or day-by-day changes? What is it they are trying to do? Where are they going financially? How do they know when they have arrived there?

The Destination and the Journey

Wealth Odyssey uses the metaphor of a journey towards the financial goals that are your real destination. I want to help you reduce your stress by showing you how to measure your success and progress relative to your *own* financial destinations on your *own* financial journey. You do not measure your progress relative to someone else's goals. Nor is progress measured relative to any market level on any given day. You need to know how you are doing for the long term as measured against yourself. In many ways, this takes some of the stress out of personal finance; you can become less influenced by the real or apparent success of others.

Some would try to calculate their financial future precisely. You cannot calculate the unknowable. Modern Portfolio Theory and behavioral economics can measure the past and our reactions to that past and can help us to determine what is relevant. However, the exact future number is not important because you cannot possibly know what that exact number will be. Do not fool yourself with precise calculations of the future. The calculation exercise tells you what the future *could* be—that is its value. You should be looking at the *range* of possibilities through these calculations instead.

You can read many books on investing and investments, but doing so puts the cart before the horse. Who just jumps into the car and says, "Let's go on vacation?" Not many do. Before looking at specific investments, you need to know what you are trying to do. What is the destination? No specific investment is used in this general discussion of what is important to you. You need to know where you are trying to go before you jump into an investment—*a mode of transportation*—in the *Wealth Odyssey* metaphor. Yes, it can take you somewhere, but is that where you are trying to go?

My goal is to help you to take a broader perspective about *why* you invest and save. There are many books available about how assets and investments work, pros and cons, and so forth. This book is addressing *why* you need assets. *Why?* Because you need to own more than you owe! And because you need the assets to provide current income—money in your checking account—once you no longer can work (health) or do not want to work (retirement).

Key Concepts: Net Worth, Wealth, Standard of Living, and Value

What does *own more than you owe* mean? It means developing *net worth*—assets minus debt. In the past, *wealth* has been defined as having more than enough to live on. That is the definition of rich. *Rich* is having *more* resources than necessary to maintain your standard of living. *Wealth* means having *sufficient* assets, or enough to maintain your standard of living. Wealth is your net worth value measured by your savings, investments, and anything else that has value. I will discuss the meaning of *value* next. Wealth answers the question: "Without a wage or salary, how long could you continue with your present standard of living expenses?" If you can say *indefinitely*, then you have sufficient wealth to not have to work. By the way, is this not the definition of full retirement? This level of wealth can be measured and determined for each of us. You can base it on your own desired or projected future standard of living. Standard of living in economics defines how well off we as a people are. Each of us has a unique level of expenditures that supports how we live individually as part of the population at large. I call that unique level a Standard of Individual Living, or SOIL. I will discuss SOIL in detail in later chapters.

Now, let us return to the meaning of *value*. You determine value by what others would pay you to acquire an asset that you own. Value is not what *you* paid, because it has no value unless someone else is willing to exchange money, or something else of value, for the item. *Liquidity* means there are many people willing to make the exchange, and you can do the exchange easily and quickly.

It seems obvious. However, when people start talking about investing, the conversation quickly turns to philosophy based more on greed than fundamental and prudent thinking. Such an investment *sub-philosophy* is more about *how* to invest. The conversation addresses *how* you might make money. It does not address *why* you should build net worth through your investments. An overall philosophy answers this most important *why* question first, and is mainly the theme of this book.

Once you establish an overall philosophy it starts to resolve the dilemma about how much is enough. Naturally, you want enough to live on. Not to be very wealthy or very poor, but to have enough to maintain the standard of how you live. Sure, it would be nice to have more, but then an insidious thing happens. *How do you determine when more is enough?* Many people have that problem now. They do not know what enough is so they crave more. Excessive spending grows out of hand. If you can calculate how much you need to maintain your current standard of living, you will know the income and asset base required to support it. If it is possible to improve on that—of course you should.

The Wealth Odyssey Road Map

As a guiding tool, the Wealth Odyssey Road Map, or WORM, is unique. I will explain the universal form of the Wealth Odyssey Road Map, and each part of the

Road Map, to help you make those decisions you are trying to make with your money. All financial topics on your mind will fall somewhere on the Road Map. Once you have read what follows, you will understand the general category or location of any financial tool on the Road Map. Once you have placed each financial tool on the Road Map you will better see how they relate to each other. You will learn to visualize your *own* Road Map, with your own standard of living, goals, and current situation, ultimately helping you visualize where you are financially and where you are trying to go.

This approach will help you to visualize what you are trying to do with your money, and is an important part of the financial planning process. Clearly, the financial industry has not explained the planning process very well for most people up to now. Interaction with people in my practice and in my classes has shown that they lack the mental map to guide them through an objective evaluation of their finances. As a result, they are confused. They are confused by individual financial issues, and by how those issues relate to each other. They are confused about how a decision in one area affects another financial area.

I developed the Wealth Odyssey model to help you determine how to manage money, that precious resource of which we all say we do not have enough. In most cases, there are too many goals for not enough money. How do you prioritize it all, finding enough money to meet all of those more important goals?

Standard of Individual Living (SOIL)

What is the basis for knowing how much is enough? It begins with understanding your current *Standard of Individual Living*. First, you need to be on track to accumulate assets sufficient to maintain your present standard of living. You also want to *protect* your current SOIL. Once you are on track to accumulate assets that could later support a higher SOIL; then, and *only* then, should you expand your present expenditures. In other words, it becomes very difficult to accumulate assets to sustain a higher future SOIL if you let your current expenditures get out of hand. People just simply spend too much now. They get used to living with high expenses, which they can only maintain by continuing to work. Alternatively, they must endure the harder alternative of cutting back on expenses when forced.

In what follows, I will diagram your journey—your individual Wealth Odyssey. I will show you how to measure progress on your journey. You will learn how to judge progress in light of your unique situation, based on *your* living standard and *your* current living expenses. You cannot measure progress on your unique journey by someone else's standards, but only by your own Standard of Individual Living.

The Wealth Rule and the Progress Line

The Wealth Odyssey Road Map works together with two other important planning devices to show your financial route and progress along that route. First, the *Wealth Rule* helps define your destination in terms of your SOIL and the financial resources necessary to support it. Conversely, it shows what living standard you are prepared to support given your situation today. Second is what I call the *Progress Line*, a means to help you chart progress on your journey. You will see the details of these important concepts in upcoming chapters. Combined, these three elements show how to set your financial course and how to monitor your course and progress along the way.

This approach differs from what you have read elsewhere. It dynamically sets goals and tracks progress towards those goals. The Wealth Rule and Progress Line measure the attained SOIL and your progress to maintain your SOIL along with your other goals. This differs greatly from measuring your progress against some impersonal standard or index *that has nothing to do with you*. Your basic goal is to maintain your SOIL, and you should measure your progress against that yardstick. Yes, if you can improve your standard of living, by all means, do it. However, then you must recalculate your personal standard and measure against this revised standard, and then ask yourself, "Can it be sustained?"

Once Read, Twice Understood

So how should you use this book? I suggest that you read it more than once. The first time you read anything you are just trying to get the concept, main points and broad overview. The second and third read deepen understanding of how everything works together and how to apply it to your situation. You should read books listed in Appendix E to gain a broader perspective and to fill in the philosophical gaps for your own personal Wealth Odyssey. You could also suggest that your friends and relatives pick up a copy of this book and read it. The conversations that you have with them once they have read it will deepen your understanding of the material and help you *all* to apply it in your lives.

PART 1

Defining the Wealth Odyssey

CHAPTER 1

Origins of the Wealth Odyssey Concept

Learn how to set the sail since you cannot control the wind.

Life is a long journey. Most of you embark upon it without a map. You may or may not know the general direction in which you are going. Either way, unexpected turns along the way can be confusing. There are detours. You can get turned around completely. When that happens, you usually ask for directions from someone else. They may not know how to get there either because they have not been there themselves. They may be just as confused as you are. They do not have a map either. They may give directions to a destination they *think* is right, based on what *they* would do, or what *they* think would be right for them. *They* are not *you*, however. It may be where they would go, but that is not where you are trying to go. They often are little to no help. Wouldn't it be nice to have a map to see where you are, and to see how to get to where you want to go?

Imagine looking down from above upon the busy freeways of Los Angeles or the busy streets of Manhattan. People are going everywhere. There is lots of activity. It is quite a mess. How do people ever get to where they are going? They have their own purpose, their own destination. The chaos sorts itself out. Each person has his or her own specific origin and specific destination. They are following a route to get there. You notice there are common routes. The overlapping routes create an illusion of order in some places, but in reality, it is chaos. Similarly, in the financial world, individual behavior of markets, investments, and other financial products appears to be chaos as well.

A Financial Road Map—Why?

Then it hits you. Your trip is different from everyone else's. You are on a common route, but your origin and destination is different. It is just like the busy L.A. freeway or streets in Manhattan. Your financial situation is different from everyone else's. Where you are in your financial life is different. Where you want to go is different. How can you determine where you are so you can determine how to get to your unique destination? Everyone uses the same streets or highways. A map shows all the origins, all the destinations, and all the routes in between.

What about personal finance? Is there an analogous *road map* in personal finance that starts at a unique origin, takes us to a unique destination, and makes clear all the steps in between? I believe there is, and it is a principal topic of this book. The Wealth Odyssey Road Map (referred to in the rest of the book as either the Road Map or WORM) brings all the financial origins, destinations, and routes together and shows how they are connected.

Why a Book on This Topic?

In many years of professional practice, I have observed four important and common problems people have when they think about their money. First, they focus on performance. What is it going to earn? How fast will it grow? This is like focusing on a bigger engine or faster car. It may cover terrain faster, but there is more risk of crashing and not reaching your destination at all. It also has nothing to do with getting to your destination; only getting there (wherever *there* is) faster.

Second, they make financial decisions every day without seeing how one decision affects another. For example, how does having auto insurance relate to having money in reserves? The reserves help pay the deductible so that loss does not go on a credit card. The reserves also allow a higher deductible, realizing short-term savings that can be redeployed to build long-term assets. People lack an overall perspective when making individual financial planning decisions.

Third, people tend to look at finances from the short-term point of view of income and expenses. Consumerism seems to be all about cost cutting, about saving money, or, what's worse, about spending even more. This viewpoint may be helpful on a fixed pension or Social Security, but this line of thought gets in the way of saving for retirement.

Fourth, a key factor in determining how you might get somewhere is how far away it is. You travel differently to go to a store around the corner versus a city across the country. It is the same with money. Your financial goal is your destination. You can also have more than one financial goal because life is a journey with stops along the way. How far away each goal is, though, determines what kind of financial instrument you should use.

The Road Map device helps to avoid or solve all four of these problems. First and foremost, the road map clearly identifies the financial destination, enabling you to construct routes for the first time with some precision. On the illustrated Road Map, explained in the next chapter, the *why* is on the right side of the Road Map. Today, most people give little focus to the right, or destination side or the Road Map. The right side shows where you want to go, and this inherently makes it clear what kinds of routes and vehicles are appropriate for getting there. As you will see, this is probably the most important part of the Road Map. Most people today do not know where to start, and do not know what to focus on.

You Are on Your Own, Baby

It is a well-known fact that more responsibility for managing money has been moved from the paternal company of old to individuals themselves. This is primarily due to the move from employer-managed pension plans, where the employer took all of the risks, and could hire professional expertise for actuary and investment components of the pension. Individuals supported by pensions only needed to worry about matching their budget dollars going out to those pension dollars coming in. The shift from pensions has immense ramifications for the individual. Individuals are now responsible not only for determining how much is enough for their entire life in retirement but also investment decisions that have their own critical consequences in this important area. He/she must serve both as actuary (calculating sums and returns necessary to provide sufficient income later) and as investment manager, bringing these returns to life.

Companies could, and still can, hire professional experts to address financial issues. People can do the same, but are reluctant. I believe this reluctance comes from the perception that, when they hire a professional, they give up all control. This is not true. People need to be in control of their destination. You and you alone, should determine what your financial goals are. The complexity of reaching those goals is why people should hire professional help.

This book describes a method to visualize what you are trying to do. Your focus should be on your destination. Once you focus on and are in control of this critical component, then seek the tour guide who will lead you to *your* destination, not theirs. The tour guide should do the trip your way as much as possible, adding experience and wisdom only where necessary, and where asked, to make the journey more successful.

The Role of Standard of Individual Living (SOIL)

To begin, you must know your own location on the Road Map. More important than an individual investment benchmark, you will measure your progress against a unique benchmark. Your benchmark is based on your unique situation; your Standard of Individual Living (SOIL). What is that? SOIL is a level of expenses necessary to support a desired lifestyle. When your income is sufficient to pay these expenses, you are earning your Standard of Individual Living, at least for the present.

Then the questions become, "How do you maintain your SOIL? How do you improve on it?" Improving on your standard of living is not the purpose of this book. That comes from bettering yourself through education and training. Resulting pay raises, promotions, or recognition from others should improve your income, which in turn improves your standard of living. However, you need to pay attention to being able to *maintain* the SOIL you are setting for yourself. Can you support today's expenses later?

People do not save enough. They increase their expenses through debt in an effort to raise their standard of living. This is a house of cards and cannot be sustained without improving income, and eventually assets, through saving and investing. The key question again: How do you maintain the SOIL you have? Can you maintain it in the first place? If not, you need to make adjustments. Otherwise you will have to work longer, possibly your whole life (failing health will eventually make this difficult). So let us get back to benchmarking. You should be measuring yourself against your ability to maintain your current SOIL. If you cannot maintain expenses, then you should reduce your standard of living *now*. Get a simpler life with fewer expenses *now*. Excess consumption grips many, and keeping it up when they retire is very difficult. The answer is to shift dollars used for today's excesses into sufficient assets to generate the dollars to sustain you later. I will discuss how to calculate your SOIL in a later chapter.

This framework addresses many of the problems explained above, and should help you to visualize all the essential components of financial planning and how these components relate to each other. It is just like a road map, an infinite number of origins, destinations, and some common routes between them. It is *universal* enough that everyone can use the same map. You need to know your destination before you decide how to plan to get there. Too many people have the cart in front of the horse when they concentrate on what they should be investing in right now. *Now* always changes!

What This Book is Not

This book will not give you specific investment advice. It will start your thought process and provide a model Road Map to guide your search for your own unique answers by giving definitions that are useful to you specifically. *This book is not about specific products or services.* Advertising and commercials lead us to think in term of products and services. The financial products manufactured today fit in the center area on the Road Map. They are like different modes of transportation you might use to get from where you currently are to your destination. You might walk or take a bike, a car, plane, or train to get to a destination. If you can determine your destination, then it is easier to determine how you might get there. For example, just as you would not take an airplane to get to a store just around the corner, you should not use stock for money you need next week.

Knowing your destination obviously helps to simplify the choice of how to get there. Do I do A or B, or both? Maybe some combination is actually going to accomplish more. Often a travel agent or a tour guide is useful. The chapter on Credentialed Advisors may be helpful here.

As author, I am playing three roles. The first is that of a *teacher*. What do teachers do? Their true role is to get you to *start* thinking about the subject. They cannot teach you everything, but they sure can point you in the right direction and help build a base to learn and discover more. The second role is that of *architect*. The architect helps you to design a blueprint to your specifications with the expertise to make sure it meets all the building codes and material requirements, and with the prospect that the finished project will be functional. The third role is *builder*. Once you have done the planning to your specifications, it does no good as a blueprint unless you build it.

Some just will not get it and will disagree with elements of this book. That does not matter to me as the author. What does matter is that *you* get something helpful and useful out of this book. Find where you are and determine where you want to go. Visualize your progress across the Road Map. Visualize what the various financial tools can do to carry you across the Road Map. The Road Map should help you if you are lost and confused as to what to do. Do not feel alone. Many others are just as lost and confused as you are. That is the purpose of this book, to provide a map so you are not lost anymore. Use the Road Map.

The Ultimate Goal

Where is it that this book is trying to take you? I have written it to take you mentally above the ground so you can look down and visualize where your money is being spent now, where money needs to go based on what you are trying to accomplish, and how the various aspects of personal finance fit together and work together to get you to your financial destinations. If you can get somewhere financially, then you can do what you set out to do in your life. It takes time for money to work; time is money. Money allows you the time to do those things you want to do.

The local area is on the left side of the Road Map. Unless you are already retired with sufficient assets (as defined later in Standard of Living and the Wealth Rule) money comes from you working and earning today. Money you earn today needs to be deployed to do things tomorrow. If you have spent it today, it only supports today's standard of living. There is no money for tomorrow's desires or standard of living. You can only spend money once. However, if allowed to grow, money can sprout other dollars too.

Ultimately, people do not want to have to work anymore, to retire. Some may not have a choice due to ill health and will have to retire earlier than planned. In the first case, dollars earned today have to make it across the Road Map for use on the right side, at the destination called retirement. In the latter case, the individual did not make it to his destination, so risk management needs to kick in and provide the assets and money he does not have.

The Road Map also provides a visual benchmark so you can chart your progress along the way. You customized this benchmark using a standard of living you specify and you do not relate this benchmark to anything else. You measure the Progress Line by your net worth. Scenic Side Trips will discuss briefly how you can manage that net worth. Finally, the Wealth Rule provides a means to calculate what your net worth can support. The Progress Line and Wealth Rule are used together to chart your progress. The Road Map puts all this together so you can visualize each component.

Scenic Side Trip 1.1: What Are Scenic Side Trips?

Most people think of only investing when it comes to topics like retirement, education funding, etc. Investing is an important component that relates to *how* to accumulate the dollars required to accomplish their goals. However, the broader topic is wealth. Along with this broader view comes the need for a philosophy, a guide that binds all the various aspects and approaches together, the *why* of what you are doing. Intertwined with a broader perspective is the need to look at specific financial topics a bit closer. With that in mind, there will be various Scenic Side Trips, or SSTs—side topics discussed as you progress through your own Wealth Odyssey. These Scenic Side Trips fit specific topics into the broader viewpoint and philosophy of wealth. Just as during a journey, you stop to look at what surrounds you now, SSTs will stop to look at specific financial topics along the financial journey. See the SST topic list in the table of contents to find these at the end of certain chapters.

Scenic Side Trip 1.2: The Work and Retirement Models, Past and Present

Most of us still think in terms of the money model that our ancestors taught us.

That model could be called *The Work Model*: You work, you are paid, and that money pays your expenses. In other words, your employer, through paying for your work, supports your expenses (your standard of living). Our parents or grandparents worked under this model, and this model still supports them in retirement as *The Retirement Model*. They worked to earn a company pension; that company pension (plus Social Security) pays them, and that money pays their expenses today in retirement. The model does not really change because their income still comes from an external source.

The work model still exists for everyone. Money comes from somewhere to support your standard of living measured by your expenses. However, the retirement model has changed. People have noticed the model has changed but they have not considered the ramifications. Where is the money *going* to come from when there no longer is an employer? (Possibly, the government will reduce its programs too). The source of income does change!

Where will the money come from if you no longer have an employer? Answer: Through the wealth you accumulate; through the assets beyond your debt; through your accumulated net worth. There is now a difference between these models. It did not matter for your grandparents, but it does for you. Thinking under the wrong assumptions, with the wrong model, will have serious consequences. You can visualize the difference between the *work model* and the *retirement model* by comparing the Road Map in the next chapter to the Road Map in Chapter 12.

CHAPTER 2

Introducing the
Wealth Odyssey Road Map.

*Delusion is continuing to do the same thing while
expecting to get different results.*

—Modern day proverb

All road maps, when viewed for the first time, appear busy and confusing. Your first glance at the Wealth Odyssey Road Map central to the theme of this book is likely to be no different. However, as you read each chapter describing each component, it will become easier to visualize, internalize, and use. The Wealth Odyssey Road Map displays your entire financial *terrain*. As with most maps, it is important to understand the terrain as a whole, but it is also important to examine individual parts of that terrain more closely. This examination occurs in sequential chapters in Part II. As you examine the whole map and each of its parts, the Road Map will become more familiar—be patient!

Unfolding the Map

At last here is the Wealth Odyssey Road Map. I have chosen to display each version of the Road Map on a full page to enhance the font size to ease your reading. I will apologize for the slight inconvenience this might cause by having to turn the book each time to view it. I think you would agree that readability is important.

Figure 2.1: The Wealth Odyssey Road Map (WORM)

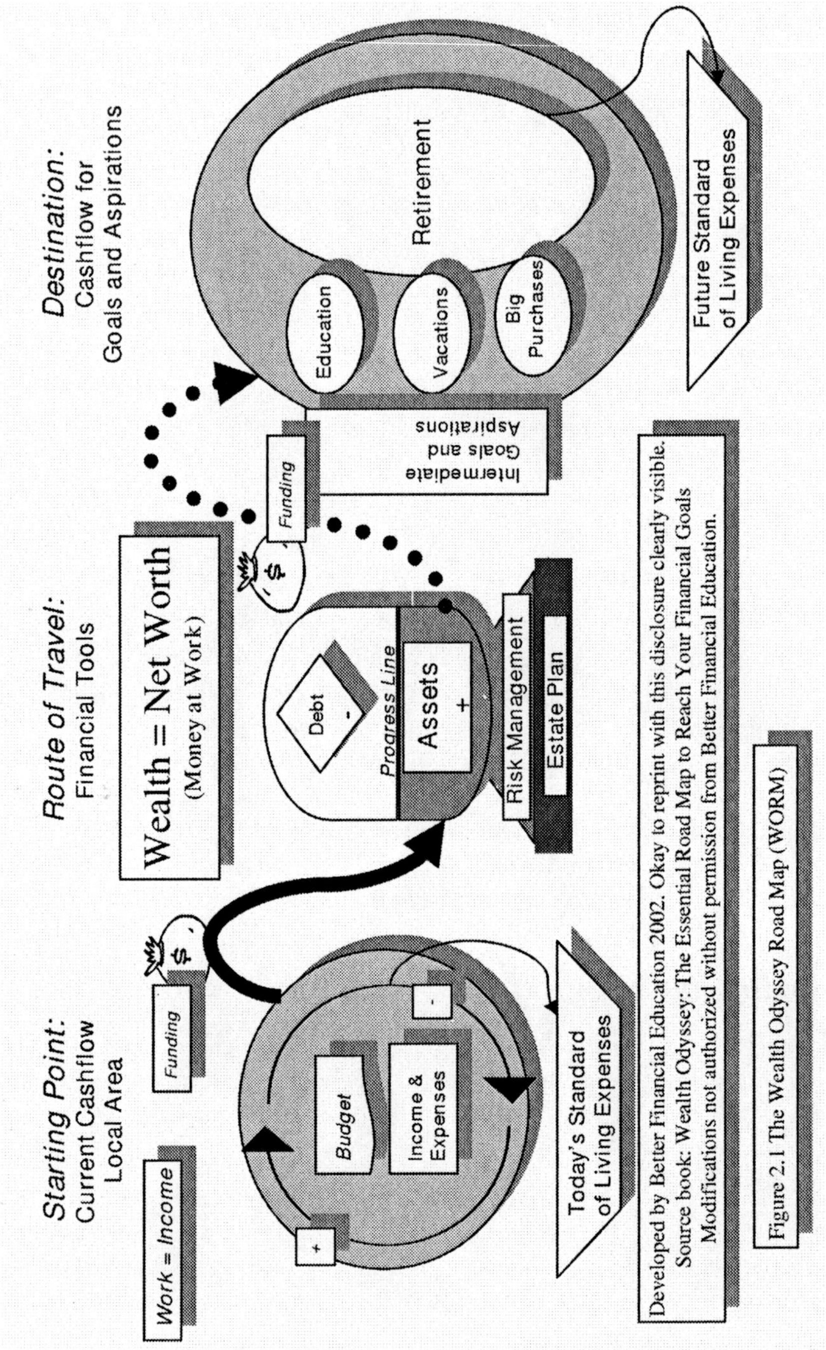
Starting Point:
Current Cashflow
Local Area
Work = Income
Funding
Budget
Income & Expenses
+
-
Today's Standard of Living Expenses
Route of Travel:
Financial Tools
Wealth = Net Worth
(Money at Work)
Debt
-
Progress Line
Assets
+
Risk Management
Estate Plan
Funding
Intermediate Goals and Aspirations
Destination:
Cashflow for
Goals and Aspirations
Education
Vacations
Big Purchases
Retirement
Future Standard of Living Expenses
Developed by Better Financial Education 2002. Okay to reprint with this disclosure clearly visible.
Source book: Wealth Odyssey: The Essential Road Map to Reach Your Financial Goals
Modifications not authorized without permission from Better Financial Education.
Figure 2.1 The Wealth Odyssey Road Map (WORM)

At first glance, there is a lot of detail in Figure 2.1, and yes, it may be confusing (I told you so!). The best way to begin to comprehend the Road Map is to divide it up into its major components: the Starting Point, the Destination, and the Route of Travel. Throughout the book, the Starting Point, analogous to your current financial situation, is referred to as the *Left* side of the map. The Destination—where you are trying to go, analogous to your financial goals, is referred to as the *Right* side. The *Center* of the WORM is the route of travel, defined at a high level as Net Worth. There is much detail inside of each of the three map *terrains*. The rest of the chapter summarizes the three terrains; Part II examines them in depth.

The Left Side: Current Finances

The Left side of the road map is analogous to the *local* area; that is, the area where you are today or where you are starting out. You are familiar with it. It is about today, the here and now, the present. Much of it is a given; there is little that you do not know about, and there is relatively little to plan for. It is the day-to-day cycle of earning, living, and bill paying. During your working years, your income is commensurate with, and roughly equals, your work. You spend that income on a variety of current needs. Most people spend what they make, most of that on current expenses. Those expenses support your current standard of living. It is all about today. Should you choose to do so, you can put some towards assets, debt or risk management—the Center and Right portions of the map (discussion to follow). These assets, debt, and risk management tools, in a limited way, serve to increase or support your current standard of living. Most important, for the purpose of this book, your Standard of Individual Living (SOIL) is measured by the amount *you* spend on today's expenses.

Because the Left side is the area most people are most familiar with, they tend to fall into two financial traps. First, they focus too heavily on what this side of the Road Map does for them. Second, they take it for granted. People focus too much on income. They think earning $200,000 a year is better than earning $60,000 a year. Yes, the $200,000 income implies a higher standard of living (supporting more expenses) than the other. However, the real question is, can they sustain these higher expenses? What wealth would be required to sustain that standard of living without having to work all the time to generate that incoming cash flow? For example, $60,000 a year with 6 percent put aside into assets for the future implies a higher sustained standard of living in the future than $200,000 a year that is spent on bills and current living expenses and little saved. Then you get a perceptive realization, dollars you *spend* today go to make *someone else* wealthy.

The Right Side: Financial Goals

The Right side of the Road Map represents your true financial destination. What are your planning goals? What are the long-term goals, in terms of future standard of living? What are the shorter-term, aspirational goals? College education? Big-ticket purchases? Travel? In other words, what is your destination or destinations? These are your financial goals over your lifetime. They define the destination, the *there* inherent in your journey, the underlying reason for your Odyssey. What is important to you? What is it you are trying to do? There may be more than one specific destination. Financial goals are set for various stages in your life. Most people spend little time really contemplating their financial destinations. Moreover, they spend even less time thinking about what life will be like at that destination. Yet, for a real-life road trip, you take much more time to familiarize yourself with your destination, to determine what you would like to do there. It is amazing how much more time the average individual spends planning vacations as compared to time spent on financial planning.

When you travel, the first question for most is the *why*. Why are you going to a specific destination? Beautiful scenery? Relaxation? Adventure? The why question is first, and drives everything else behind what makes the trip happen (the *how*). Yet few seem to ask this question about their money. They just start to do things with it with no specific answer to the why question, no specific contemplation of the destination. There may be many different planning goals, some closer in time than others. Once you determine where you want to go by answering the why question, then you can determine how to get there. Finally, you can begin to accumulate the resources in the form of assets to make it all possible.

When you travel, the mode of transportation used depends on how far away the destination is. As you get closer to any destination, you may change the mode of transportation. For example, with many long-distance trips, you change from an airplane to a rental car and then finally walk when you have arrived. Therefore, distance to the destination becomes a key factor in determining how to travel. How long is it before you need those dollars to achieve any of your goals? With money, time is distance. The kind of asset, or vehicle, chosen for those dollars differs based on the period for each of your goals or financial destinations. This is the key.

The Center of the Map: Net Worth

The Center of the Road Map represents the *how*. Following the analogy, these are the routes and *modes of transportation*. Traveling modes may include planes, trains, autos, bicycles, or foot. Travel modes for financial assets include investment classes such as cash, savings, stocks, bonds, metals, commodities, real estate or other real assets, or mutual funds comprised of any of these. What will carry you to your financial destination most effectively? How will you get *there*? The *how* employs assets and debt. In life, you use multiple modes of transportation when you travel, so it follows that you should use multiple modes (investment classes) for your assets too.

Also as in life, there are hazards along any journey. These hazards vary by mode of travel. How do you deal with those? How do you plan to meet these hazards if presented with them? This is known, in real and in financial life, as risk management. On the other hand, what if you are successful and ultimately reach your goals? Estate planning properly manages your assets once you are unable to. Both risk management and estate planning provide a foundation for your modes of financial transportation—your assets.

Viewing the Map as a Whole

Many people spend all their *financial* time and effort concentrating on the center of the Road Map; that is, trying to make the most of their investments with no longer-term destination in mind. Worse yet, they may spend their life concentrating on the Left side—spending everything for today and trying to get more and more income to spend. When they invest, it is with the point of view of making money. How much money is enough? Strategies and tactics out of touch with goals usually do not work.

Without a destination in mind, the goal becomes making more money. However, the goal should be to increase wealth. There is a subtle distinction, but an important one. Wealth can support a standard of living and may make work optional. This point of view places the importance on what that money must do in the future—so you do not spend it prematurely. You need to build wealth. You have to own more than you owe. In addition, you need to build enough wealth to support *your own* Standard of Individual Living, not that of someone else. When is there enough money? This is like focusing on building a faster racing car. Performance is all that seems to matter. It is about getting there fast. It does not really matter where *there* is so long as you go fast and best everyone else. Without a destination, you are wandering and it is easy for you to get lost. Making money and spending it keeps you on the Left side of the WORM. You never accumulate the assets necessary to reach your destination goals.

Wealth is net worth. Net worth equals assets minus debt, as illustrated in the Center of the Road Map. Stated differently, your net worth—your *wealth*—is equal to everything you *own* less everything you *owe*. Net worth is the all-important focal point on the map that few pay attention to. Why? Because most people consider income, the Left side of the Road Map, to be what is most important. Aren't most of today's financial success measures based on income? The reality is that it is the Center of the Road Map that carries you to your destination. It is wealth that is central to your success.

Failing to grasp the importance of wealth causes you to have to live always on the Left side of the Road Map, where work equals income, equals expenses, equals standard of living, with nothing left over. Repeatedly, people forget that high expenses follow high income. They forget that they will want to sustain that standard of living—or even improve it—later in life. How? People say they want to retire and not have to work anymore. Retirement is a destination on the Right side of the Road Map. To get there, you have to go through the Center (unless you want to work full time until you die). You need to have modes of transportation in the form of varied assets comprising net worth sufficient to carry you to your financial destinations.

I am not talking about inventing new money here. People want to learn how to get somewhere without having to do anything. Neither this book nor any other has the secret of accumulating assets without effort. Trips require effort, and you have to make the effort to make the trip. There is no instantaneous way to leave one place and get to the other side. New money comes from your efforts. It comes from working, from expanding your skills and knowledge, and from your adroit use of all of the above. You learn how to be more efficient working. Similarly, you need to learn how to be more efficient with your money. It means, among many other things, reducing the wasted dollars dripping through your fingers without thought.

The Earning-Saving-Spending Formula

Many financial formulas are simple. One example is the basic budgeting formula. Most people *incorrectly* think the budget formula is Earnings – Spending = Saving, because this is how most people budget. This formula implies that they save *what is left* after Spending needs are met. Look at the Road Map, note that *Earning* and *Spending* are on the Left side, while the *Savings* part of the formula targets money into the Center of the Road Map as funding for Net Worth. If you target what concerns you first, then budgeting is as simple as making sure dollars go there *first*—first to the Center of the Road Map. Therefore, the correct formula is Earnings – Saving = Spending. This is what the formula looks like when you *pay yourself first*! Then you can spend the rest comfortably knowing that you have addressed the important things first. To build wealth, it is more important to keep track of the dollars going to the Center of the Road Map, not the dollars going to the Left, at least in specific detail. Then, you will someday arrive at your destination. This is budgeting with a purpose, budgeting that may get better results in the end.

It is okay to spend money. That is the purpose of money. However, it is not okay to spend money if there is nagging concern about not accomplishing goals. Now it is interesting to note the *road to ruin formula* that many use in practice: Earnings – Spending + Debt = No Savings. In other words, use Debt to support Spending, and Save what remains, which on a *net* basis is zero. This is how many people budget today. Those using this formula will find they will have to work all their lives to generate the money needed to pay expenses. Spending your financial time keeping track of all your expenses on the Left side does not accomplish as much as putting focus on the Center. Are you putting some money into the Center of the Road Map? Are you accumulating the wealth needed to support *your* standard of living? Recall that wealth in this book does not mean queen of England wealth. It means the amount of assets needed to support *your* expenses as dictated by your Standard of Individual Living.

What If You Own Your Own Business?

How about someone who owns his own business or company? Is the formula any different? He should view himself as an employee who is paid, therefore work equals income. That income then flows through this same Road Map just as with any other employee. Cash flow comes out of the business to support current Standard of Individual Living defined on the Left side of the Road Map. Diversification becomes especially important (see Scenic Side Trip 2.1 below). Business owners get caught in the trap of managing only one asset, their business. They forget about diversification principles. Yes, the business itself is an asset and is part of the Center of the Road Map. It may help them get to their destination on the Right side of the Road Map. However, should the business slow down, not only has a concentrated asset position declined in value, but income has been adversely affected—a double whammy. It is helpful to visualize what is happening in such a case by remembering what part of the Road Map applies.

Scenic Side Trip 2.1: What is Diversification?

Diversification is *not* chasing the current popular asset class, that which produces comparatively attractive returns. If you are chasing returns or chasing yields, it is a sure sign you are not diversified. Chasers are 1) too focused on what is hot now, and 2) often burdened by losses in what was most recently hot. Both are bad, and usually lead to poorly returning asset portfolios.

So what is chasing, anyway? Take any investment. The cycle starts with the recognition of rising prices for that type of investment. It might start with stocks, and then switch to bonds, then to gold, then to real estate, then to crude oil, etc. The point: You keep chasing after what is hot, chasing after what appears to be going up. Why does that happen? Because the crowd is chasing attractive yield or returns—they are trying to make maximum short-term money. Chasing is fueled by two very human emotions—greed and fear. Greed is euphoria fueled by over-confidence. Fear is panic fueled by lack of confidence. Fear and greed are both ends of a spectrum; prudence lies in the middle. Placing money in what's hot now is often no more than speculation, while *investing* is placing money in a diverse portfolio containing several prudent investments. What happens at the final emotional crescendo of such behavior? People cannot make decisions and sink into financial gridlock. They cannot diversify at the market top because they would have to pay taxes, and they cannot diversify at the market bottom because they cannot take the losses. We cannot undo the biology of human emotion. It has taken millennia to develop our emotional reflexes to our environment. In only a blink in evolutionary time, we have had to contend with a challenging and rapidly changing market environment, when emotions often mislead us. You must fight such emotion with rational information. Your thought processes need to be such that you set up your assets so you do not have to watch them constantly, but only monitored at a high level.

So what, then, is diversification? It is a rational approach to placing money in many different baskets. Some baskets are in favor, while others are simultaneously out of favor. Given time, the market baskets will switch, and we will not have had to do anything! We already had the diverse market baskets in the portfolio. Why do markets switch? They switch because the markets' emotional moods change and the crowds follow. If we keep chasing market baskets driven by emotion, we then have to change the baskets constantly. Only by sheer luck will we succeed.

Unless lucky, we will all make mistakes. To avoid, or at least reduce, the number of such mistakes, it helps to diversify among different types of investments. This lowers risk, and lowers what statisticians call *standard deviation*. Standard deviation measures the variability of possible returns around a projected or desired outcome. Returns that are channeled in a narrower range (lower standard deviation) often generate more dollars in the long run than returns that occur all over a wider range. It is in the mathematics.

Scenic Side Trip 2.2: Family and Friends Helping Family and Friends

It is with the best intentions when friends or family attempt to provide financial guidance to their friends or family. However, this can lead to trouble. You might choose to explain to a family member what you are doing with your finances. Indeed this might be right for you. However, it assumes the other is in the same situation with the exact same concerns, goals, priorities, and resources. In other words, your assumption is that they are living in your exact same location on the Road Map and have the exact same destinations as well. The fact that they are family and friends strengthens this assumption. You assume therefore that the exact same modes of transportation would also be appropriate. Is this true?

Clearly, this is not necessarily true if you think about it. As a result, although it might be nice for someone to know what you are doing financially, it might not be appropriate for him or her. Only *they* can determine how to get to their unique destination from where they are at now.

Be careful giving, and accepting, help and advice, however well intended.

PART II

Components of the Road Map

CHAPTER 3

The All-Important Destination

---

*What is the use of going fast, if it is in the wrong
direction, not towards the desired destination?*

What is the financial planning issue most people overlook? It is the most important question they should ask themselves, yet most people do not. When teaching personal finance classes I am often asked loads of questions during the class breaks. What kinds of questions do students ask? No surprise—most are about financial vehicles we just learned about: the financial products, strategies, and tactics—the details (nuts and bolts) of their own special financial performance (sports car). For example, they ask me after talking about retirement plans, "Should I do a Roth or a Traditional IRA?" They ask me after talking about saving for education, "Should I do a 529 plan?" I am not faulting people for asking questions they have on their minds. The marketing and sales environment has conditioned them to think about just the topic raised. People are conditioned to think about the products that solve their concerns; yet they have not adequately determined what their concerns are, or what their priorities are among those concerns. Worse yet, they tend to change their focus when a new topic comes up. Few ask the first logical question about their destination, about their *needs:* What are you trying to do? Where are you trying to go?

The answer to this question is called the *Destination* on the Road Map. Everybody has their own destination in mind when it comes to their money. However, very few people actually think about what their concerns and goals are and prioritize them so that they can allocate their money wisely toward accomplishing them. If they have not done this critical process, then there is a risk of never arriving at the destination. In regards to retirement, never arriving means working your entire life.

Figure 3.1: Wealth Odyssey Road Map: The Destination

Destination:
Cashflow for
Goals and Aspirations

Retirement

Education

Vacations

Big Purchases

Future Standard
of Living Expenses

Intermediate
Goals and
Aspirations

Funding

Route of Travel:
Financial Tools

Wealth = Net Worth
(Money at Work)

Debt

Progress Line

Assets

Risk Management

Estate Plan

Starting Point:
Current Cashflow
Local Area

Funding

Budget

Income &
Expenses

Today's Standard
of Living Expenses

Work = Income

Developed by Better Financial Education 2002. Okay to reprint with this disclosure clearly visible.
Source book: Wealth Odyssey: The Essential Road Map to Reach Your Financial Goals
Modifications not authorized without permission from Better Financial Education.

Figure 3.1 The Wealth Odyssey Road Map – The Destination

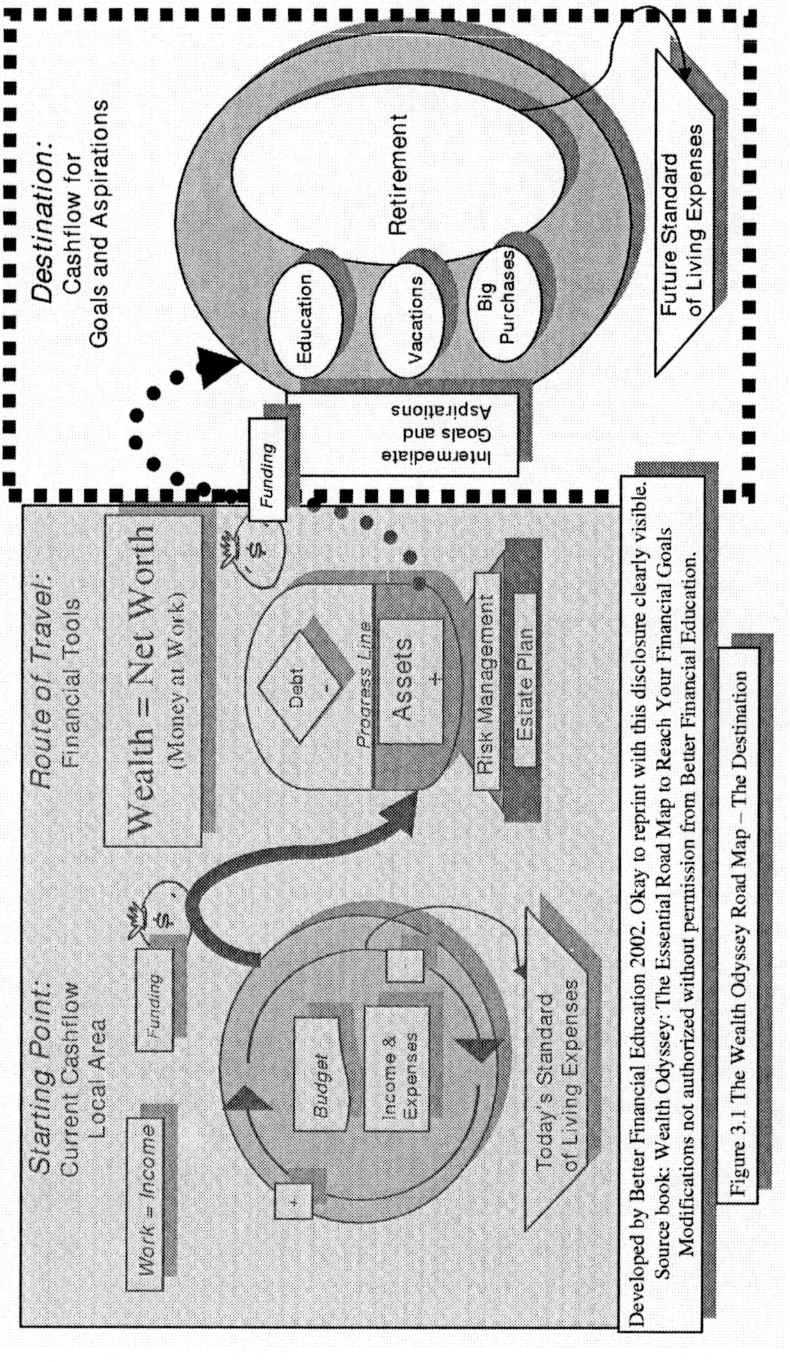

Destination Specifics

Destination is represented by the Right side of the Wealth Odyssey Road Map in Figure 3.1. The destination is where you are trying to go with your money. What are your concerns and goals? Will you have enough to retire? Do you want to help with your children's education? Are vacations important to you? Do you have aspirations to start a business, take a sabbatical, or downshift in your busy life? Is there a job change or career shift coming? Do you have big purchases in mind: a nice car, vacation home, boat, or home remodeling? All of these needs require having the money to do them. Yet few people address how to be sure they put savings aside to accomplish and arrive at these destinations. The money needs to flow from the daily budget into the Asset Reservoir so when you arrive at the intermediate and final goals the money is there to accomplish them. Let us examine how this planning is done.

Consider how planning is done in the military. There are many targets but limited resources. With money, there are many things you want to do, but limited resources. So, let us break it down as in military planning. First, there is the overall objective. There are *campaigns* to address sub-objectives. There are *phases* to address the timing of each sub-objective. *Contingency planning* addresses what might go wrong, or not according to plan. Additionally, the plan looks at what to do if things go right.

What is your overall objective? Answer: to arrive at your destination. The most important destination most people have is to be able to retire someday. Because it is the main objective, resources need to be applied to accomplish it. Campaigns address sub-objectives. Examples of sub-objectives include providing for education for your children or grandchildren, a vacation, or the purchase of a new car.

What are the phases of the campaign? Answer: the time sequence of dollars applied to those goals that come first, second, and so forth, all the way to the biggest and last goals. Note here that the priority may go to the last campaign, but there may be many phases between now and then. Why is this important? Because the resources go to the high priority goals, not the goal that comes along first chronologically! Higher priority goals need to be funded first, while lower priority goals may not be funded completely. You have limited resources, which mean you cannot do everything. You need to prioritize.

Contingency plans include risk management and address those things that could go wrong. What if you lose your job? What if there is injury, illness, or death? What assets are at risk of loss? From where would that risk of loss come from? What if things go right? Answer: estate planning. Now you have succeeded, what happens now?

Remember that a key question driving your financial planning throughout is what is the Standard of Individual Living you wish to sustain in the future? Put another way, how big does the retirement circle need to be on your WORM? The college education circle (choice of schools—Ivy League versus community college) clearly reflects standard of living. What kinds of big purchases do you have in mind? Are these to be purchased during or after your working life? All of these factors figure in to nailing down the specifics of your destination goals. Get out a pencil and paper, and start listing *what* and *when*. We will get to the *how much* question in just a moment.

Taken all together, there are two main challenges in developing the Right side of your Road Map. First is condensing your many goals into a few critical ones so that you can apply resources efficiently to accomplish them. Second is quantifying and prioritizing these goals so that they become actionable. Quantifying goals involves what I call the Wealth Rule, and prioritizing them requires a careful evaluation and soul searching for what you, and your family, really feel is important. Remember, to determine your goals and aspirations is the critical first step since these are *why* you are going there with your money. Goals and aspirations are on the Right side of the WORM. *How* you accomplish those goals and aspirations is to travel through the Center of the WORM. So let us get to the *how much* question now that you have determined the purpose of the money.

Running the Numbers—The Wealth Rule

The single largest looming issue for most people is retirement. The common problem I have observed in my business is the inability for people to determine *when* or *if* they can retire. I am always asked one of two questions, depending on how soon the person wants to retire. If they have time before they are going to retire, they ask, "When can I retire?" If they are getting ready to retire now they ask, "Can I retire now?"

The Wealth Rule is a method to help people determine how much they need in assets to achieve the largest of financial goals. Most of the time it is used to calculate retirement needs. We will come back to the Wealth Rule in risk management in Chapter 7 as well. I developed the Wealth Rule based on numerous research articles published over the years in *The Journal of Financial Planning*, an industry publication of *The Financial Planning Association*, and other academic research into the question of how long can money last when it is withdrawn with fluctuating balances. A list of those research sources is in Appendix F. Using the Wealth Rule, the person asking, "When can I retire?" can answer: When I have saved this much. The person asking, "Can I retire?" can answer: If I can live on this much. What is *this much*?

Based on this research, the maximum annual withdrawal rate should not exceed 5 percent of the total assets base. The assumption is that money withdrawn will be replaced by current returns on that asset and the *net-net* may be zero; that is, the asset may be preserved at its current level, or may even grow if returns are modestly better. This is a long-term perspective, since there will likely be negative return years as well. How to handle negative returns is beyond the scope of this discussion. Briefly, prudent reserves for such years are suggested. Consulting with a credentialed advisor familiar with these studies is also suggested.

Many financial planners use 4 percent annual withdrawals as a rule of thumb for planning. A lower withdrawal rate can extend even longer how long money would last; therefore, this is a more conservative rule. These are the big issues for retirement—how long will the money last? The answer is: With enough assets and a well-managed withdrawal rate, as long as you live! If you match withdrawals to percentage of value, it does not matter how long you live, because the withdrawal is not enough to withdraw everything. However that is too perfect a world to expect, so you must plan for variations in the plan, and make some accommodation for how long you expect to live. Since we cannot manage length of life, we must manage asset base and withdrawal rate, and their possible contingencies, instead. It is especially prudent to take as small a withdrawal in the early years of retirement since research has also shown that large declines in market values has the worse effect on retirees if the decline occurs in the earlier years of retirement. The withdrawal rate can always be adjusted higher later in retirement years when the length of time needed for sustained withdrawals is less than 20 years or so—but length of life is still a gamble so withdrawing too much still has a risk of depleting the assets.

With this background, we can see how the Wealth Rule works? The purpose of the Wealth Rule is to help you determine how much you need in your Asset Reservoir in order to retire. It starts with your current standard of living. I should make a note that as your standard of living changes with promotions or pay raises you need to recalculate your own Wealth Rule. The same is true should standard of living decline. I want to reemphasize this because it is the inherent power of the Wealth Rule: the ability—and need—to recalculate what needs to be in your Asset Reservoir any time your SOIL changes. You do not need to worry about how much you might spend in the future because the Wealth Rule will calculate your required Asset Reservoir for the future based on today. It self-adjusts. If SOIL changes, recalculate what the Asset Reservoir needs to be. The relevant standard of living is how much you spend each month today.

Many planners suggest using 70 to 80 percent of your pre-retirement income as a starting point. I disagree with this rule of thumb as I have yet to meet someone about to retire who is voluntarily willing to reduce his standard of living by 20 to 30 percent! See Scenic Side Trip 3.1 for further discussion on determining your SOIL. This rule of thumb originates with people not adequately planning ahead of time, and thus they are forced to reduce their expenses when they retire. It also comes from experience with old-fashioned pensions that automatically pay a retiree less than current earnings; if the retiree did not save to make up the difference, then he or she is forced to cut expenses. However, proper planning can prevent one having to reduce expenses, or allow him to reduce them over time rather than suddenly on the day of retirement. If you can reduce expenses today then two things happen. First, you can use the extra dollars to reach the retirement goal with which you are struggling. Second, the retirement goal is easier because the expenses you are trying to support later are less.

For now, let us say your Standard of Individual Living expenditures are $70,000 per year. Once retired, you may or may not have a pension, but there is Social Security. Suppose for this example you estimate an income of $10,000 per year from Social Security. Using the Wealth Rule's 5 percent withdrawal rate calculation, how much needs to be in the Asset Reservoir to continue to pay $60,000 ($70,000 minus $10,000)? Sixty thousand divided by 5 percent (.05) equals $1,200,000. That becomes the target Net Worth (Center of map) required to support the lifestyle and standard of living in the Retirement portion of the Destination (Right side of map). It is how much you need in this specific situation with which to retire. If you want more assurances the money would last longer (you have a family history of longevity) you can use some percentage less than 5 percent. For example, 4.25 percent would require $1,411,765 ($60,000 divided by .0425). This is the *this much* amount I talked about a few paragraphs ago. If you are retiring in the future, are you saving enough to accumulate *this much*? If you are retiring now, do you have *this much*? As you will see in Chapter 5, you must not forget that you will be taxed on retirement plan withdrawals too.

In summary, the Wealth Rule helps you answer the question about how much you need to retire at the same standard of living you have today, or a different standard of living if you choose. If you do not have that amount saved, then you need to save more, delay retirement, or downshift the standard of living. One final comment: The Wealth Rule helps you determine the amount of money you need. It does not address how you invest that money or how you need to adjust the withdrawal with changing values because of fluctuating economies and markets.

Running the Numbers—Intermediate Goals and Aspirations

Unfortunately, there are no convenient rules of thumb that I am aware of for calculating lump sum destinations such as college, vacations, a new car, or other big purchases. That is because many of the factors are more variable for shorter-term goals. The largest variable is the uncertainty of returns over shorter periods. Even conservative investments, such as savings accounts, vary. The savings balance does not vary; it continues to grow with interest. However, the interest rate paid can vary, sometimes considerably, driving a different future value.

For intermediate goals and aspirations, I suggest using calculators found at most financial websites. To get a better understanding of the basics, *The Everything Personal Finance Book* (Adams Media, 2003) has good tables and explanations to do these types of calculations.

Returning to SOIL: Tying in the Wealth Rule and the Progress Line.

I will continue to develop your understanding of SOIL in the coming chapters. SOIL is the foundation to planning your journey across the WORM to retirement. You need to be able to determine your starting and ending points to connect the two and successfully make your financial journey. SOIL does this. Once you know your own SOIL, you can approach the problem of determining how much you need by using the Wealth Rule, which tells how much you need to accumulate in your Asset Reservoir. Knowing this, you can answer your two most important questions: How much do I need to retire? When can I retire? Finally, the Progress Line, which will be introduced in Chapter 5, will allow you to measure your progress. I bring this all up here so that you can observe how these concepts are linked together as you read on about your Wealth Odyssey.

How Do You Determine What You Will Need to Retire On?

Let us take the most perplexing issue—that of determining retirement needs. First, should we always consider retirement first? What about a goal coming up sooner, like college education for a child? It comes down to this: Who will lend you money for retirement? Answer: Nobody. College loans are readily available, but there is no such thing as a *retirement loan*. Therefore, retirement should be a higher priority, hence more heavily funded goal. For retirement, rather than speculate on what you might live on in the future, start with what it is you are living on today! That is your current standard of living. Most people envision a retirement in which they maintain at least the standard of living they have today.

So assume that today you are working and earning $60,000 per year *gross*. You are putting 10 percent away into the company retirement plan, or $6,000 per year. Social Security tax is $4,000. Finally, you pay federal taxes of $9,000 plus $3,000 state income taxes. What is your current standard of living? In other words, how much are you spending to live the lifestyle you are living?

$60,000 – $6,000 – $4,000 – $9,000 – $3,000 = $38,000 net? Or,
$60,000 – $6,000 = $54,000 net?

Figure 3.2: SOIL (Standard of Individual Living)—Today and In Retirement

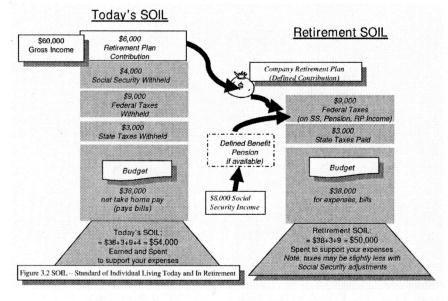

From Figure 3.2, you can see in this case that $54,000 is the level of expenditures applied to your current Standard of Individual Living. Why? You did not spend the $6,000 that went into the company defined contribution plan yet. It is still yours! All the rest of the money has gone to pay for today's expenses of some kind. Standard of living is measured by *all* the money you spend to support your lifestyle. The taxes in this example were also *spent*. You did not notice this because they were withheld from your paycheck.

You would apply the Wealth Rule to $54,000: Dividing by 5 percent, (.05) requires an asset base in the Asset Reservoir of $1,080,000. However, this is not considering other sources of income in retirement. How much will Social Security be? In this example, suppose it is $8,000 per year. Is there a traditional pension payment (from a defined benefit plan)? In this example, let us say no. In addition, as a refinement, since there is no longer a wage or salary, there is no longer a Social Security tax. In this example, that was $4,000. Now $54,000 minus $4,000 leaves $50,000.

Because $8,000 will come from Social Security, $50,000 minus $8,000 gives $42,000 of SOIL expenses that the Asset Reservoir needs to support. If there were additional money coming from a defined benefit pension, then you could reduce the withdrawal from your assets further. $42,000 divided by .05 gives a final retirement base of $840,000 after adjusting for not paying Social Security taxes but instead receiving a Social Security payment. You would make the same calculation adjustment for a pension. You would also ignore the Social Security adjustment if you do not qualify for, or do not want to plan on, Social Security.

Compare this calculated number to what you have in your current Asset Reservoir. Your Asset Reservoir is in the center of the WORM and is the imaginary container in the diagram that needs to fill up with assets to support you when you reach each of your intermediate and long-term destinations. Are you trying to retire today? If your Asset Reservoir is not full, you need to evaluate further your retirement decision. Delay retirement until you do have it full? Are there other expenses you do not need in your budget?

Let us work the Wealth Rule in reverse to show how it can be used alternatively. Let us say this person has saved $500,000. Reversing the Wealth Rule, 5 percent (.05) times $500,000 equals $25,000. The current balance might support this expense level for retirement, or for a distribution starting today. In our example, this person would compare the $25,000 to the $42,000 to determine if he could reduce his spending by $17,000 in order to retire now.

Bear in mind cost of living increases. You need to balance your asset accumulation needs with your asset consumption needs in retirement to keep up with inflation. In addition, if your standard of living goes up while you are still working, you need to save more to support that, too. You accomplish this before retirement by investing more of each pay raise, bonus, and promotion and getting as good a return as your comfort with risk will allow.

All of these complexities are very good reasons to consult with a credentialed advisor to work out the many alternative scenarios. Further, the Wealth Rule helps you determine what you would need to retire. It does not tell you how you need to invest those assets properly.

Scenic Side Trip 3.1: "I'll Be In a Lower Tax Bracket When I Retire."

Another common statement I hear in class: "When I retire, I'll pay less in taxes."

I am going to challenge your perception of income taxes now. Taxes are based on spent income. Stated differently, income that is not spent, is not taxed. Recall the $6,000 contribution in the example above. It was not spent, but put into assets to be spent later. And it will be taxed later when it is spent on future standard of living expenditures. Therefore, I challenge your point of view that taxes will be less when you retire. You are taxed today on the money you actually spend to support your SOIL. In order to reduce taxes you need to reduce income. To reduce income you have to reduce your standard of living. Is that really what you want to do?

This is an important point, because the money you take out of your company plan, or Traditional IRA, etc. will be taxed. Why would you take the money out of these retirement plans? To pay for the expenses that supports your standard of living in retirement. Remember our example above where $42,000 needed to be taken from a retirement plan to meet expenses. That withdrawal is taxed along with Social Security and/or pension income. If you have the same level of expenses in retirement as you have today, count on your taxes being the same also. It is wishful thinking to say your taxes will be significantly less. Think of the income tax as a standard of living tax instead.

CHAPTER 4

Back To the Beginning, Current Finances

If you don't change your direction, you are likely to end up where you are headed.

—Proverb

It may seem a little counterintuitive to start with the right side of a map, move to the left side, and then end up in the middle. Yet, just as with many a road trip, that is how the Wealth Odyssey works. Identify the destination, then work back to where you are, then diagram the routes in between. You *start with the end in mind,* and then fill in the details to get to that end. So here the focus changes from Destination to Origin; that is, in the Wealth Odyssey metaphor, the Left side of the map. This portion of the map represents your current finances and day-to-day money management.

Without going further, here is the trusty WORM again in Figure 4.1. This time the focus is drawn toward the Left side, where you are today, the *local area.*

Figure 4.1: Wealth Odyssey Road Map: The Local Area

Developed by Better Financial Education 2002. Okay to reprint with this disclosure clearly visible. Source book: Wealth Odyssey: The Essential Road Map to Reach Your Financial Goals. Modifications not authorized without permission from Better Financial Education.

Figure 4.1 The Wealth Odyssey Road Map – The Local Area

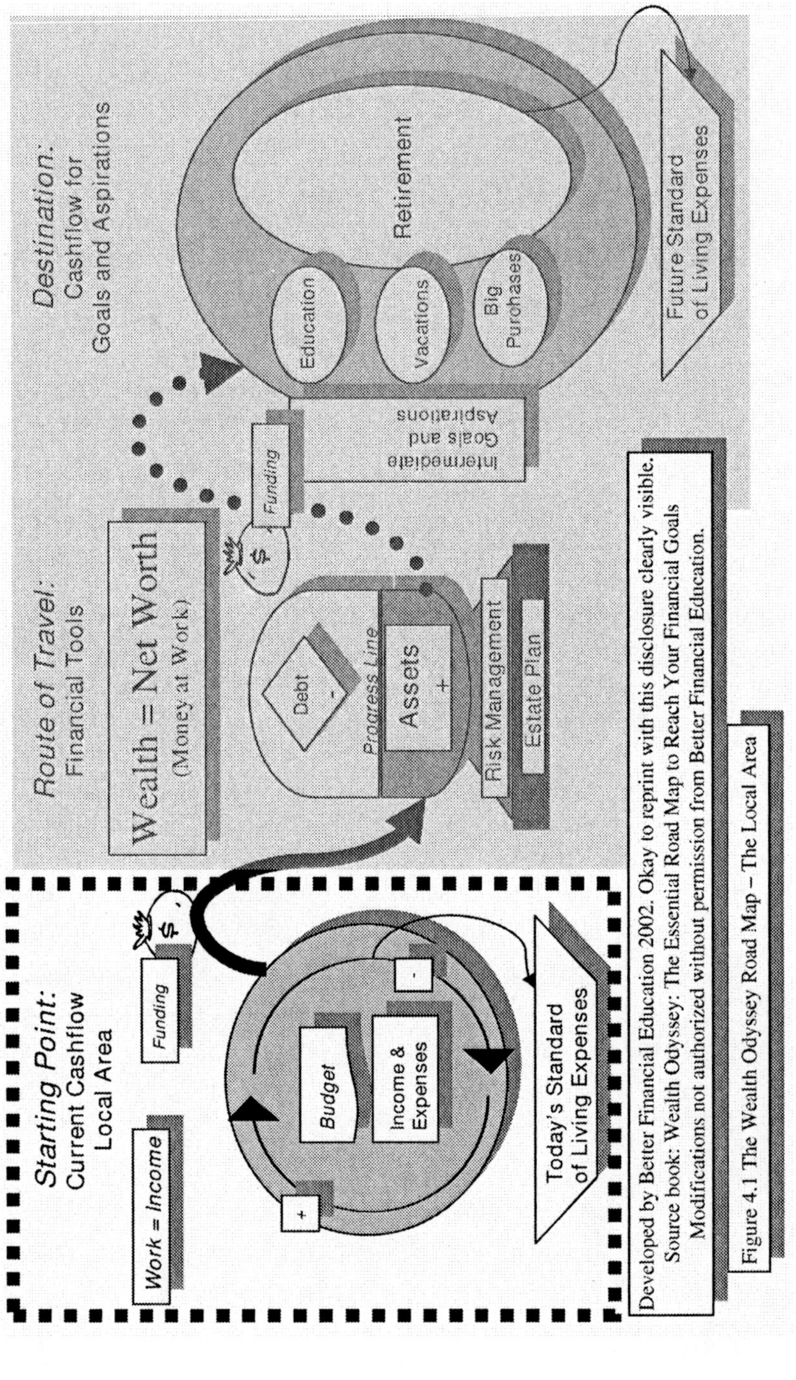

For most of the time, for most of us, work has equaled income. You spend the income from work on various expenses. Those expenses support your standard of living. Standard of living can therefore be measured by your expenses. The Local Area on the Left of the Road Map presents this cycle of income and expenses. The size of the circle depends on your standard of living.

Now the key question: "Where does the money come from when you are not working?" Most people have not thought this through. "I put a few dollars away," they say, but they are more concerned about today's expenses and standard of living than they are about tomorrow's. Thus, they make a major decision about their future standard of living without serious thought.

Another result of this mode of thinking is viewing *everything* as an expense. The result: important things, like building wealth in the middle of the Road Map compete on an equal basis, or with even less priority, than current bills. These are not equal in importance. The center of the Road Map, if managed properly, represents those dollars moved into categories critical to achieving Destination goals. One of the major goals most people have is not to have to work for those dollars anymore.

The Funding Formula

The Earning-Saving-Spending formula (Earnings – Saving = Spending) surfaces again. The Earning-Spending cycle is clearly depicted on the Left side of the Map, while Saving should follow the heavy curved line, called Funding, into the Center of the Road map. Most people spend almost as much as they earn, however, saving very little. Some even withdraw what little they do save. The classic example of this is the person who contributes to the company retirement plan, and then withdraws the money to deal with a job change.

Naturally, people hesitate to follow the Funding line in Figure 4.1 because it means not spending today. It means a reduced standard of living today. Without thinking, those who fail to save are forcing upon themselves a reduced standard of living in the future, because the resources are not there to support the expenses later. This means they have to keep working to produce the necessary income to support their expenses. They hope health holds up to support this have-to-work cycle, but what if it doesn't? How do you maintain your standard of living if the future cash flow from working is reduced? Proper planning and shifting a few dollars into the Center of the Road Map today is how it is done.

What about Debt?

It is worth mentioning debt, and more will become known in Chapter 6. Some people try to increase artificially their standard of living through debt. When this happens, the formula transposes to Earnings – Spending + Debt = (–) Savings. Of course, the net result usually reflects no dollars saved, and more often, accumulation of debt. The formula becomes Earnings – Spending = Debt. If this pattern continues, debt ends up exceeding assets. Result: negative net worth. When dollars earned in the future are needed to pay off yesterday's consumption, the Progress Line towards sufficient Net Worth is held down and the Asset Reservoir is kept from filling to the level sufficient to meet future goals. These folks *owe* more than they *own*, and they are headed for a very lean retirement standard of living unless something changes.

Towards Asset-Driven Thinking

All this leads to an obvious conclusion: Perception needs to shift from *income-based* thinking to *asset-based thinking*. Assets provide the dollars needed when you are not working. Assets become money working for you. While you are working today on the Left side of the Map, you are like your own asset producing dollar returns for your efforts. *You* are working for *you*. What is this income as an asset worth? Take your annual gross income and multiply it by how many years of work you have left. Once you see this number, risk management comes to mind again. How do you protect this large asset?

The Income Replacement Model

Recognizing the gradual shift in income sources required by the different stages in your life is one of the key concepts underlying the Wealth Odyssey. When younger, you have relatively more energy and career growth opportunity and relatively fewer assets already on your personal accounting books, so your expenses—your Standard of Individual Living—are supported mainly through current income. However, as you get older, and particularly when you reach retirement, you support a greater portion of your basic needs, including things like increased medical expenses, by your assets. To a degree they are also supported by income replacement tools such Social Security and withdrawals from retirement plans (retirement plans are part of your assets, except for defined benefit plans). The details and timing are unimportant here; what is important is to grasp that eventually assets must replace your wage earning power in order to maintain your Standard of Individual Living. This is illustrated in Figure 4.2.

Figure 4.2: The Income Replacement Model

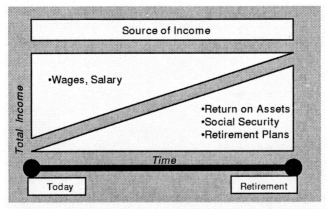

Figure 4.2 The Income Replacement Model

The All-Important Role of SOIL

The fundamental question then becomes Standard of Individual Living. What supports your standard of living? Today, and tomorrow, when there is no income? Standard of living is your local area, your benchmark. Just as everyone lives in their own space called home, everyone has their own space called Standard of *Individual* Living, a standard unique to *you*. This is SOIL. How you maintain that standard of living, both today and in the future, will be unique to you. If you ask someone else, he or she will base their answer on the perspective of their own standard of living. They will answer based on their own local area on the Road Map. Work maintains your unique standard of living today. What will maintain your standard of living if works stops, either voluntarily or involuntarily?

Importantly, expenses drive your SOIL, not income! Income is how expenses are paid. What expenses? Those tied to your unique standard of living. How much of your money you are spending is what determines your standard of living. It is not income. If you borrow to spend even more, then you have increased your standard of living on borrowed money. Now you are in the dilemma of paying yesterday's expenses as well as today's expenses, leaving even less for the future. If the money is not there from assets, then work is not optional. You still have to work to bring in the income to pay your standard of living expenses.

What If...?

The focus of the Left side of the Road Map is income and expenses, with (hopefully) a funding flow moving towards building wealth. It is all about cash flow. Cash flow supports the monthly budget, and in turn, standard of living. While working, jobs are the usual cash flow source. However, what supports standard of living when there is no income? What if there is a job loss, an abrupt or planned transition? An injury or illness? Retirement? A sabbatical? People make the mistake of spending pay raise and promotion dollars on a higher standard of living without considering these possibilities, let alone their longer-term destinations and their inherent needs. How do you simultaneously save and invest efficiently while you enjoy living today? How do you take extra dollars today to focus them on sustaining tomorrow's standard of living? Answer: Recognize that income is, in itself, an asset, and it should be managed *for keeps*. How much of it are you going to keep? How much are you going to give away to increase someone else's wealth? That is an important topic of the Left side of the Road Map, and it is a critical connection to the Center of the WORM where funding of these concerns occurs. Goals such as disability income insurance, building adequate reserves, and debt reduction come to mind. There is no one right answer for everyone. The WORM helps you make your own personal, but more informed, decisions.

Scenic Side Trip 4.1: What Wealth Supports You?

The wealth of the economy supports everyone. The wealth or earning power, of a company is a subset or part of that economy. It has always been the wealth of that company—the cash generated from company sales—that supported its workers, from top management on down. Your participation in the company's wealth occurs through each paycheck.

Pension plans also require money to come from the cash flow generated by company sales. Traditional pension plans are called defined benefit (DB) plans. DB plans provide an income to company retirees as long as they live. Government employees' pensions are also set up this way, except the money comes from current cash collections of the government (taxes), and not through pension plan investments as in the corporate world. DB plans are what can truly be called *pension* plans. Indeed, this is the concept I mean when I use the term pension since the retiree knows the benefit amount.

So in DB pension plans, where does the money come from for the retiree's paycheck? From investments made long before by the company into the pension plan and earnings realized since then on those investments. Investments in what? In companies that made up, and currently make up, the economy. The pension plan management calculates assumed rates of return. Why? If you know you will owe $50,000 each year to a retiree beginning in 20 years, you assume a certain amount of return on the money invested each year to realize enough assets to pay that retiree. If the pension plan earns less interest, the company has to put in more money to make up the difference.

What does this have to do with your situation? It provides a model for your own Wealth Odyssey, which may indeed be carried out in part through your 401k plan. 401k plans are called defined contribution (DC) plans. Other plans work much the same way (403b, 457, Roth, IRA, Simple IRA, Sep IRA, etc), in deferring money for retirement. You know the contribution amount, but not the future payout, which is determined by real-world investment returns that are any-thing but a given. True, you can estimate the payout, and unlike defined benefit plans, you can make the calculations. In fact, you *need* to. This is a major differ-ence between the *old* DB and the *new* DC plans. You must make these estimates yourself, or do it through a credentialed advisor.

Between DB and DC plans, what stays the same? For one thing, the dollars are invested in the same economy and in the same markets. The example of $50,000 needed in the future requires the same adjustment by you in your 401k that com-panies make on DB plans when returns are lower than expected. Everything still depends on the same economy. This is true globally. What is the moral of the story? You cannot avoid the economy or its effects on you. You are under its effects right now. The challenge is to understand and learn to use economic forces to drive your wealth, and not be left behind.

The stock market is a barometer of the economy, a consensus of opinion—not fact. It could go one way or another or in a way totally unforeseen. It becomes fact only after events have happened and the consensus has responded. The markets do not necessarily truly reflect the facts of the economy in the short term, since they are trying to place money where they *think* things will go in anticipation of economic and business cycles.

Scenic Side Trip 4.2: Budgeting.

The topic of budgeting brings visions of 1) laboriously tracking each expenditure and 2) setting limits on spending. What has been lost is the basic question of "What is money for?" It is to spend! However, we all recognize that spending everything foolishly leaves nothing for needs that are more serious. Hence, budgeting was born.

A budgeting approach should include a practical balance and compromise between spending needs and desires, a set of limits and a plan to achieve important saving and investment goals. How can this be accomplished? By reversing the typical budgeting exercise!

The typical individual looks at where each penny goes; determines *where else* that penny might be placed, and makes sure that penny gets there by setting limits on spending elsewhere. Then he or she tries to *save what's left* for other savings and investing needs down the road.

There are many problems with this. First, the long-term needs are given last priority; therefore, it is no surprise what few pennies are left after everything else. It is no wonder it is so hard to save for anything. Second, this concept of budgeting is based on the philosophy of denial. I cannot spend more than this here. I cannot do that, or I will not have money *left over* for this. This is all based on limits, on negatives, without any positive reinforcement or goal achievement. Then third, if the process is not laborious and full of sacrifice, we feel we have not accomplished anything. So how does reversing this work?

It starts with addressing your concerns! What are your financial concerns? List them all by brainstorming and get them all down on paper in front of you. Long-term concerns. Short-term concerns. Intermediate-term concerns. Then prioritize these concerns. What is important to you? Once you have concerns listed and prioritized, what do you see emerging as goals? Goals address concerns. Then dollars address goals! This is what *pay yourself first* really means. Get dollars *automatically*, again automatically, every month going towards addressing the accomplishment of your current, higher priority goals. By addressing goals *automatically* and *first*, and *every* month, you address your concerns slowly but surely.

This *pay yourself first* becomes Earning − Saving = Spending. This takes that nagging pressure off. You achieve goals, and the rest of it works out. There is a reward at the end of the process, and you feel better. Furthermore, you feel better about what you *do* spend. Who cares how you spend what is left? That is what money is for, to spend. To spend on today's needs once enough is set aside to meet the spending concerns you have for the future. Nevertheless, it only works by doing the process in reverse! It is not a constant exercise in denial, but becomes one of fulfillment. It needs to happen *automatically* so you are sure important resources are not spent accidentally or impulsively. It is a proper allocation of resources to meet tomorrow's needs and needs for today as well. You will find that soon you can live *within your means* and feel good about it!

Scenic Side Trip 4.3: What is a Retirement Plan?

Many people have the impression that having what their employer provides, or their own IRA or Roth IRA, means they have a retirement plan. No. People call these retirement plans, but they are not *plans* at all. They are the vehicles to accumulate the wealth needed to support your standard of living once retired. However, just having one does not mean you have a retirement plan! Where is the *plan* part? What must these dollars do in retirement? How do you know when you have enough? Where do these dollars come from? There is no *plan* unless you plan it!

A retirement plan means that you have actually planned! You develop a plan by evaluating all the concepts in this book. For you have to be able to establish an overall destination; to be able to establish how you are going to get from where you are to where your destination is; to be able to monitor your progress along the way on that journey; and finally, to be able to say you've arrived at the destination! A plan means that there are definite steps that you have evaluated and taken. What is your retirement *plan*? Do not be fooled into complacency by the company label of "retirement plan." It is just another tool to build wealth in your Asset Reservoir.

CHAPTER 5

The Center of the Road Map, Assets as Modes of Transportation.

Your greatest gain is not what you get but what you become.

—Unknown

We have seen that money coming in can be at risk. In other words, income is at risk. What happens when your income is interrupted; job loss, health issues, disability, planned transitions? Really, is not income loss what happens at retirement too? Where is the money going to come from if income stops? Mainly it comes from two sources. One source is the tools of risk management, which provide income coverage if things go wrong, discussed further in Chapter 7. It is natural that you plan primarily on everything working out as planned. As we all know, things happen and plans are changed. However, for most of us in most situations, the main source where money will come from when income stops is *net worth*. What is net worth? Net worth equals assets less debt. In other words, it is everything you own less everything you owe. It is what is remaining after everything else is spent and you have paid off all debts. It is what so few people today pay attention to. That is surprising since it is the main source of vital future income.

The Asset Reservoir

You can see that the center of the WORM looks like a jar or container, with assets at the bottom and debt at the top. Like air, debt can fill the entire container, meaning (relatively speaking) that nothing is there! To the extent possible, you should fill the reservoir with Assets. As with a reservoir behind a dam, from which water is released slowly over time as needed during the dry season, assets in your Asset Reservoir are accumulated and stored whenever possible and you release them over time as needed.

The Progress Line

The Progress Line on the Road Map measures the amount of assets relative to the amount of debt. In general, the closer a *full* Net Worth Progress Line is to the top, the better. In other words, the farther upwards the Progress Line moves, the closer you are to achieving a goal by filling the Asset Reservoir This means that assets have overcome debt. The Progress Line is figurative. It does not actually exist. However, Net Worth, the amount you own less the amount you owe, measures it. Debt on the Road Map is above the Progress Line. It impedes getting to your goal. More debt pushes the line downward, thus keeping you farther from your goals on the right of the Road Map. Less debt moves the line upward to fill the Asset Reservoir, which will get you closer to achieving your goals. You can visualize on the Road Map what debt does to both the Progress Line and reaching any destination in Figure 5.1. We can see there are two components to net worth. Assets are what you own. Debt, more technically known as *liabilities*, is what you owe. This chapter discusses assets and the next chapter discusses debt.

Linking the Concepts: SOIL, Wealth Rule, and Progress Line.

The importance of the linkage between your own Standard of Individual Living (SOIL), the Wealth Rule, and the Progress Line cannot be emphasized enough. As mentioned in Chapter 3, your SOIL today is your point of reference to where you are today, financially. It is critical to be aware of it so as to be able to successfully travel to, and live in, your future. Once you know your SOIL, you can use the Wealth Rule to calculate what you need to accumulate in your Asset Reservoir. The Progress Line helps you monitor how well you are doing towards reaching your established retirement destination, while plugging in other intermediate goals and aspirations along the way.

Working through the linkage it is possible to know today what amounts of assets you need in your Asset Reservoir to retire on later. Because you know this, you can answer those nagging questions "How much do I need to retire?" and "When can I retire?" You can answer these questions for your own unique situation:

"When I have accumulated the amount I need based on my SOIL." Knowing this number, you then can make smarter choices about how to use money today. You can *pay yourself first* to be sure to accomplish what is important when the time comes. As your SOIL changes (it would change upwards with promotions, pay raises, or change downwards with pay cuts, or job changes, etc.) you recalculate with the Wealth Rule the new amount needed in your Asset Reservoir. When you get extra money and try to decide what to do with it, you can look at the Asset Reservoir and Progress Line to determine if you are ahead of or behind your goals. Based on the priority of your goals, you can make informed decisions and know what impact that will have on progress on your journey across the WORM if you spend the money today rather than put the money into your Asset Reservoir.

The Source of Assets

Where do assets come from? They come from what you do with your current income dollars. You saw that money and wealth starts on the Left side of the Road Map. You saw that income comes from work. Your choice is what to do with that income. How much of that income do you spend on current standard of living expenses? How much of that income do you transfer to the center of the Road Map, where assets reside? Which assets do you utilize? That depends on the answers to the destination questions found on the Right side of the Road Map.

How do you get to any destination? That depends. Asset dollars are those you direct to future standard of living expenses on the Right of the Road Map. Everyday bills, etc., on the other hand, is money directed to current standard of living expenses, those on the Left of the Road Map.

Figure 5.1: WORM: Net Worth and the Progress Line

Destination:
Cashflow for
Goals and Aspirations

Retirement

Education

Vacations

Big
Purchases

Future Standard
of Living Expenses

Intermediate
Goals and
Aspirations

Funding

Route of Travel:
Financial Tools

Wealth = Net Worth
(Money at Work)

Debt −

Progress Line

Assets +

Investments

Checking
Savings
Reserves

Risk Management

Estate Plan

Starting Point:
Current Cashflow
Local Area

Funding

Work = Income

Budget

Income &
Expenses

Today's Standard
of Living Expenses

Developed by Better Financial Education 2002. Okay to reprint with this disclosure clearly visible.
Source book: Wealth Odyssey: The Essential Road Map to Reach Your Financial Goals
Modifications not authorized without permission from Better Financial Education.

Figure 5.1 WORM Net Worth and the Progress Line

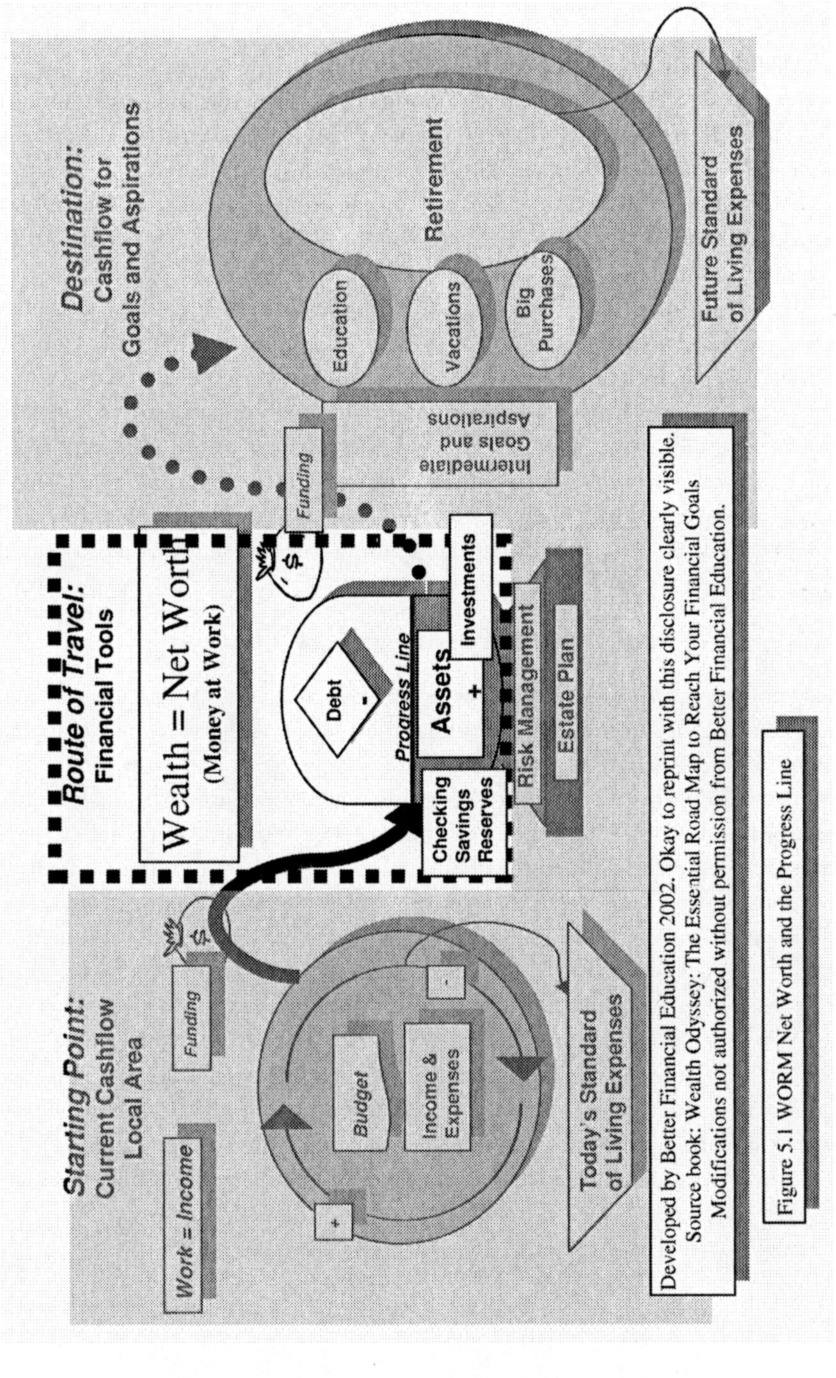

The main source of assets, not surprisingly, is *you—and your work*. Another source is your money itself—it works and produces income too.

How can your working be an asset? If you make the mistake of viewing just the local area, or Left side, of the Road Map, all you see is income and expenses. If you recognize that over a year income adds up to a considerable dollar amount, then you begin to recognize that the source of assets is income. In addition, you can view income itself as an asset. You just do not treat it that way. For example, $3,000 a month gross income is $36,000 a year. After 10 years, that is $360,000. If you spend it all, if you give it all away, you have nothing left. No asset. *It has all gone to make others wealthy.* If you shift a little to the Center of the Road Map, to the safe haven of the Asset Reservoir, it is still yours. It remains there, working as hard as you have assigned it to, until you eventually move it from the Center of the Road Map and spend it, ideally on standard of living expenses related to your destination or other financial goals you may have along the way. Nevertheless, many people pull assets prematurely and spend them on current standard of living expenses. These dollars never make it to the destination. Now they have to start all over again. Why? They have moved their progress line down, away from the destination, because asset dollars are spent before arrival at the destination.

Modes of Transportation: How to Get There

Once you know your eventual destinations, you can make smarter choices about modes of transportation to get you to that destination. What is a key factor? How far away is that destination? How long will it take to get there? How long will the money remain in that asset before you ultimately convert it back to cash that you spend on standard of living expenses? Think of length of time as the length of the journey to the destination, to the goal. You need to choose modes of transportation appropriately. You use short-term modes for closer destinations, middle for middle-, and long-term modes for destinations farther away. As a reminder, this book will not go into great length discussing any investment. You can find that information in other books written specifically about any type of asset. This book is also not about any specific investment strategy. Those topics can also be found in other texts (see Appendix E for further reading suggestions). This book discusses an overall philosophy and method of putting all the financial pieces together to work in unison on your Wealth Odyssey. Some of those pieces include the various *types of* assets you can use as modes of transportation on your journey.

Short Term Assets

A closer look at the Center of the Road Map would reveal various asset categories: checking, savings, and reserves. Although these assets are in the Center of the Road Map, you will notice they are closer to the Left side. They tend to be spent sooner, rather than later. That is okay because that is for what they are for. However, reserves tend to be overlooked. When something comes up, which it always does, where does the money come from to pay these unexpected bills? Debt! Why does it usually come from debt? Because, money for those unexpected expenses has not been set aside in reserves, or these additional expenses have not been budgeted in the current SOIL on the Left side of the Road Map. Something always seems to come up. The all-important asset vehicle known as *reserves* helps to address these unknowns.

Cash

Cash is spent on current standard of living expenses. It may be placed in the Center of the Road Map. However, it often is not left there very long. For purposes in this book, cash is 1) currency, 2) checking, 3) savings, and 4) any liquid reserves. The cash modes of transportation earn little to nothing. That is okay, for we do not want to take the risk it may be worth less when we spend it. In order to earn something, risk needs to be taken. Risk is the source of greater return. Cash is a near-term mode of transportation to be spent in the near term. That is what it is for, either to be spent some time soon or held in reserve for unexpected expenses.

You spend checking account money over the course of time between paychecks, whereas savings accounts are mainly for money that will—or may—be used within a year. People put money into savings accounts to keep it from declining in value and earn a bit of interest for a short period of time. Ultimately, you may utilize savings for a current expense, an expense that supports the current standard of living.

Liquid Reserves

The purpose of liquid reserves is to create a necessary Emergency Fund. The Emergency Fund amount depends on two factors. First is the stability of your job. If the job is stable, then income is less at risk of being interrupted. It is even better if there is a benefit through an employer that ensures that if income is interrupted due to injury or illness, the income continues to be paid. However, do not get too comfortable with employer benefits, for the employer can change them. On the other hand, they may change when you change employers. If the job is seasonal, or not as secure, then more needs to be in reserves.

Often one hears about three to six months of basic expenses in an Emergency Fund. It should be more if you work only 10 months of the year. How else do you save up for the two months you are not working *plus* the two months you have used from reserves? If you are consuming reserves, they will eventually run out unless you replace what you use up. How do you replace reserves when there are interruptions? You still have the current standard of living to support. The longer the period of *potential* interruption, the greater number of months should be in reserve. Notice I said *potential*. If you do not have the reserves to begin with, you are already behind. All travel, including your Wealth Odyssey, requires planning ahead, not reacting. Start by building reserves.

The second Emergency Fund factor is the size of your expenses. What are the minimum bills and expenses that you must pay to avoid interrupting your necessary transportation, food, shelter, and clothing needs? The size of the emergency fund should be the result of multiplying the necessary number of months times the minimum expenses that have to be paid.

You should determine what your own situation is and what your comfort level is. This helps determine the dollar amount that needs to be in your liquid reserves. Moreover, there can be different accounts, *laddering* the modes of transportation for near-term and long-term possible expenses. Laddering is a method that staggers the timing when dollars become available, a common strategy with CDs or bonds. For example, CDs that come due every three months for a year, would stagger one three-month CD, one six-month CD, one nine-month CD and one 12-month CD, which would time the money from the CDs to be available every three months.

The mode of transportation used to keep liquid reserve dollars then depends on two things. First, we do not know when, or even *if*, we will use these dollars. Therefore, you should not be so conservative with your deployment that these dollars are not working hard enough. On the other hand, you could use these dollars in short order, so you should not take a lot of risk with them either. Short-duration bond funds are one type of asset vehicle that could be used here. Duration is a measurement of time. It also is an indication of how prices of bonds will react to interest changes. Example, duration of 3 years means generally that a 1 percent change in interest rates up could produce an approximate 3 percent decline in value. A credentialed advisor should suggest an appropriate specific mode if this confuses you. See Appendix D on selecting a credentialed advisor.

Investments

The purpose of investing is to put dollars into assets that work harder, and produce more return, than cash assets. People argue over the different financial tools available for use, but for our purposes here, the tool you need is one designed to get you to your destination. You use different modes of transportation to get to different destinations. Closer destinations use different modes than destinations that are more distant. If the money is going to be spent sooner (a closer destination) the correct mode of transportation is slower (cash tools). It the money can be left working for a longer period of time (a more distant destination) the mode of transportation can be faster (stock, long-term bonds, commodities, real estate, or tangible assets). Why? Because they need to be given sufficient time to work correctly. As such, Investments are located to the right hand side (closer to Destination) on the WORM.

It takes time to get to a desired destination. Rushing time by trying to go faster means you are taking more risk. The risk in this case is that something is not going to work according to plan. To reiterate, long-range destinations require long-range modes of transportation. Short-range destinations require short-range modes of transportation. A commercial airplane cannot work correctly getting you to the local store. It can work correctly getting you to the other side of the country. People have lost sight of this. Why? The perspective of trying to make money has clouded things. It is important to match the asset to the length of time needed for the asset to work properly. Investment modes of transportation are tools manufactured for your use in the financial services industry. A general rule of thumb: Use the long-term investing modes for dollars that are not needed for five years or longer, because they need time to work properly.

You must also consider *liquidity*. Liquidity is the ability to convert back to cash if needed. Again, a credentialed advisor is highly suggested to help fully understand the relevance of liquidity to their investments. The point that confuses people sometimes is having too much liquidity and losing site for what the asset is. Just because something is liquid (easily sold) does not mean it should be viewed as a short-term investment. For example, stocks are liquid, but are not necessarily a short term-investment. The liquidity brings with it the possibility of substantial loss. Lack of liquidity also could be a problem. If you have invested with a long-term intention, but then something changes, either in the market or with your goal, how do you retrieve your money?

In review, assets are the mode of transportation to carry you to the financial destinations that represent your goals. You go through the Center of the Road Map to arrive at the destinations on the Right. The mode of transportation should fit the timing of the desired arrival at the destination. Time here represents distance to your goal. Otherwise, the resulting mismatch increases the risk that things will not work out as planned.

Sure, someone needs to give attention to how you get to a destination. I do not think that should be you. Use what is already manufactured; do not reinvent the wheel. You do not need to concentrate on building the airplane or the airline. That is not your business. Your business is deciding the destination and getting yourself aboard. You find the proper mode of transportation already manufactured for your destination based on how far away that destination is. Your focus is to do what you do best—your own job, then to monitor progress to your destination at checkpoints along the way.

Scenic Side Trip 5.1: You Live in an Anthill, Not in a Matchbox...

You depend on the electric grid, utility grid, sewer grid, water grid, transportation grid, food grid, gasoline grid, road grid, business grid, and so forth. You depend on myriad other people; it is not just you in your house. Your own matchbox actually exists inside an anthill. That anthill represents everyone else and the interconnections of the economy. Our economy and other economies globally are interconnected.

Many believe that investing in the economy is too risky. Perhaps some of the confusion comes from not knowing the difference between risk and uncertainty. Yes, many things are uncertain in any market. It is uncertain what the future value of a home will be. However, one could also argue that it is more risky not to invest in a market. Historically, the stock market has kept ahead of inflation. By not investing, the risk is that the purchasing power of your dollars falls behind due to inflation's effects.

You already participate in the economy just from living in it. You are interdependent on other people. You depend on other people to build and others to distribute the car you drive to work, others to build and distribute the parts that made the car, others to build and maintain the roads you drive on, etc. You depend on others to be at work for you, to work with you so that your work also counts, and they depend on your work so their work counts too. You depend on other people to build and still others to maintain the power grid that keeps you warm, cool, or dry. You depend on others to build and distribute the batteries that power your watch, and still others to build and distribute the watch that serves to keep you on time; others to grow and distribute the food you get at the grocery store, and to work at that store so that food is there when you need it. For anything and everything you do, you depend on others. That fact has been taken for granted.

Depending on others is what makes an economy work! So, how does this affect your wealth? How do you participate? The obvious way is through your income. You work for money. However, your money can work for you too by providing the fuel—the capital—to finance companies and their projects. The success of companies and their projects is reflected in the economy. The markets reflect the success of the economy, which is a reflection of successful companies and their projects. Therefore, by investing, you make money work for you. Once you get money working hard enough, then you do not have to work as hard. Time is money—the old saying—but more money also means more time. More time for you to do things you would like to do, rather than have to do. The objective is to build wealth! Wealth is not defined as Bill Gates wealthy, but enough money to support your standard of living.

Scenic Side Trip 5.2: A Summary: The Economy as Source of Wealth

The goal of investing is to capture the underlying growth in the economy as it is reflected in each market—capital markets, such as stocks and bonds; real assets and commodities, etc. This reflects in turn the assessment of all the market participants as a whole. The goal is to capture the trend, *not the daily fluctuation*, in the growth in wealth resulting from a growing economy. You do this by investing in the markets and through diversification and asset allocation in as many markets as you can. You do this globally because each economy is separate to some extent, and is growing at a different rate. People often confuse the subject of the economy with the subject of the markets by mixing the use of various terms and concepts. Figure 5.2 provides a simplified matrix to help you separate the two topics.

Figure 5.2: The Relationship Between the Individual and the Economy

The Relationship Between the Individual and the Economy		
	INDIVIDUAL	ECONOMY

Source of Wealth	•Wages and salaries
	•Market returns on capital
		•Labor force growth
		•Technological Progress
		•Productivity enhancements
		•Economic activity
		  •Consumer spending
		  •Business spending
		  •Government spending

Role of Markets	•Allocate capital •Place value on ownership •Measure combined individual perception of economy	•Reflect success of companies •Place value on economic activity

Relevant Terms	•Bull and Bear Market
	•Bubble
	•Bust
	•Capitalization
		•Expansion
		•Contraction
		  •Recession
		  •Depression
		•Inflation
		•Deflation

Figure 5.2 The Relationship Between the Individual and the Economy

The markets reflect the economy. You cannot separate yourself from the economy. You already participate in it through your work, the salary you receive for that work, and that portion of salary that you spend back into the economy. You can expand your wealth by participating in the economy even further by participating in the various markets; that is, by investing your *capital*, not just you labor, into the economy. This participation provides the capital for companies to grow. As companies grow, so does the economy. As the economy grows, that wealth is reflected back into the assets that support that economy, and into your wages.

This is a simple explanation. Economics is beyond the scope of this book, and the market interaction with the economy is continually under study to get a better understanding of the dynamics. The economic texts and the texts on investment philosophy in Appendix E would be helpful to read to understand this dynamic interaction more. My purpose here is simply to separate the terms and concepts that often are used incorrectly, or are often confusing unless you understand what the term applies to, the economy, or the market.

Scenic Side Trip 5.3: Liquid Reserves.

People get into financial trouble by not having enough reserves. Sure, people have money saved and invested, but it is not always liquid. *Liquid* means you can convert it into money without penalty. Theoretically, money in IRAs, 401ks, and other retirement-oriented accounts is accessible. However, withdrawals are subject to penalty prior to the tax code's specified age for penalty-free withdrawal. In addition, because people have this overriding concern for not having enough to retire on, they get myopic and put *too much* into retirement accounts. Where is the money we need when injury, illness, job loss, or reduced working hours inevitably comes along? People tie up their money. When they access it, more evaporates to penalties. Of course, they must pay deferred income taxes too.

So keeping sufficient reserves outside of retirement-oriented plans is important. That money can be oriented as conservatively or as aggressively as you want. However, by having reserves, we avoid the penalty for early access. Once you are beyond the tax code's age for penalty, then retirement money is accessible. That is what it was for to begin with! This implies you have two destinations for which you need to plan. One is retirement, for which you use retirement-oriented modes of transportation. The other is the unexpected, for which liquid reserves—*just in case* emergency money—is the appropriate mode of transportation.

Because of the penalty, it costs more to build reserves in retirement-oriented accounts. Would it not be better for you to build reserves so you do not pay the extra penalty? Why reward the government for your poor planning?

Almost as bad, people borrow on their credit cards. This costs more and puts on an additional payment burden just when you cannot handle the burden.

Once you have determined your minimum monthly dollars need to sustain a budget in an emergency (for example $3,000 a month), you multiply that by the number of months that makes sense for your situation and/or comfort level (for example 10 months—if your job is not secure). The result is the dollar amount you say you should have in reserve (this example: $3,000 x 10 = $30,000). You can save these dollars as conservatively or aggressively as you feel prudent and comfortable with. However, the issue really is having them set aside in the first place. The bottom line: It is better to consider liquid reserves as a separate goal.

CHAPTER 6

The Center of the Road Map, Debt

Change occurs in the direction of our attention. We create change by paying attention to what we want more of, not to the problems we want less of.

—Psychology-Appreciative Inquiry

You saw earlier that net worth equals assets less debt. You have just read about the asset section in the middle of the Road Map. Debt is above the Progress Line. Debt stands in the way of reaching your destinations. That is why it is placed between assets and your goals on the Road Map. Debt sucks dollars away from your standard of living. Debt creates the illusion of progress because it creates a higher standard of living sooner than it can be sustained. Those expenses have to be paid. The problem is trying to pay off yesterday's standard of living at the same time you are trying to maintain today's standard of living. The problem is impatience. However, as you will see in this chapter, not all debt is created equal.

Figure 6.1: WORM: Debt and Net Worth

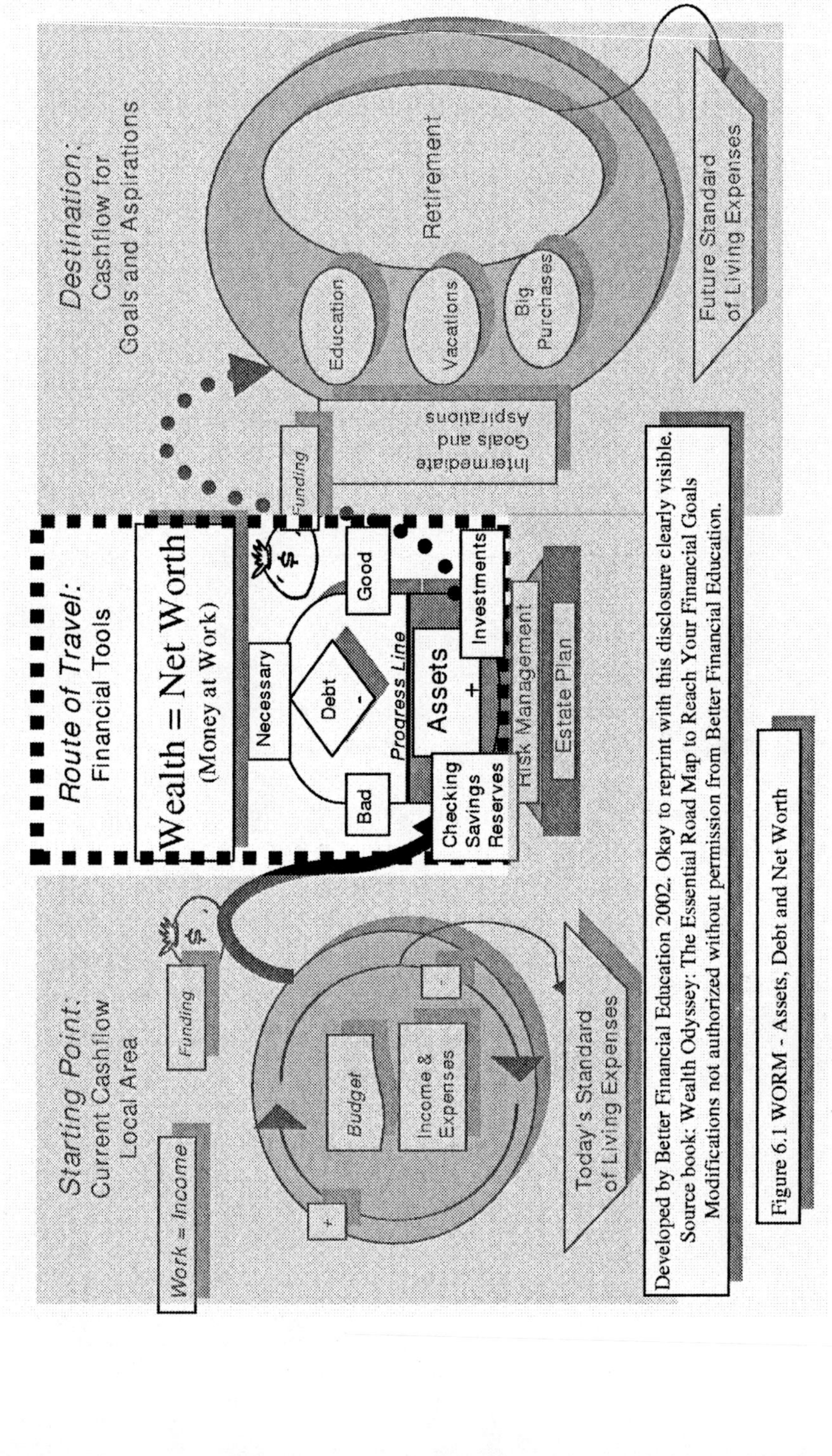
Starting Point:
Current Cashflow
Local Area
Work = Income
Funding
Budget
Income & Expenses
+
-
Today's Standard of Living Expenses
Route of Travel:
Financial Tools
Wealth = Net Worth
(Money at Work)
Necessary
Debt
-
Bad
Good
Progress Line
Assets
+
Checking
Savings
Reserves
Investments
Risk Management
Estate Plan
Funding
Intermediate Goals and Aspirations
Destination:
Cashflow for
Goals and Aspirations
Education
Vacations
Big Purchases
Retirement
Future Standard of Living Expenses
Developed by Better Financial Education 2002. Okay to reprint with this disclosure clearly visible.
Source book: Wealth Odyssey: The Essential Road Map to Reach Your Financial Goals
Modifications not authorized without permission from Better Financial Education.
Figure 6.1 WORM - Assets, Debt and Net Worth

Take a look at Figure 6.1. In the WORM model, Assets accumulate below the Progress Line, while most debt impedes getting to your destination. Debt stands between the financial goals of your future standard of living, and where you are today with your current standard of living. Most debt creates the illusion of a better standard of living. If properly controlled, debt can improve standard of living over a long period of time. For example, a mortgage is long-term debt used to purchase an asset that will retain or even increase in value. However, out-of-control debt means standard of living actually has to go down in order to pay back the out-of-control expenses from a previous excessive debt expansion. Balance has been lost, and it is likely that the Asset Reservoir will not fill.

If all your focus is on debt, debt is all that you will have. Why? Because without you giving proper attention elsewhere, you can achieve nothing else except that to what you have paid attention. In other words, how can you have assets if there is no focus on building assets, while instead you place all attention on debt and its reduction?

The financial services industry uses the term *liabilities* when talking about debt. It means the same—it is what you owe. The purpose of debt is to enhance your standard of living today, but you do it by borrowing on your future income. You need to take care also with these modes of transportation, which is to match the debt mode to the timeline for which consumption will take place. If there is a mismatch, things do not work out as planned, just as with the mismatch in modes for assets.

Debt allows an increase in today's standard of living by spreading the use of money over time. You direct debt dollars to today's standard of living expenses. These dollars go to the Left side of the Road Map. You can use debt to get to a destination correctly, when matched with the correct time horizon, or incorrectly, when debt is mismatched and uncontrolled. Let us see how this works.

The Good, the Bad, and the Necessary

For purposes of this book, there are three kinds of debt: *good*, *necessary* and *bad*. Most people lump all debt into the bad category.

Good Debt

Good debt is used to acquire an asset that goes up in value. An example here would be debt incurred to buy a home. It matches the time of payment with the use and value of the asset. You should not purchase a home if you will own it for only a short period. In general, the five-year rule for long-term assets applies here as well. Constant moving requires selling and buying. These costs eat away at the growth prospects of the asset. For shorter duration stays, most people find that renting is likely to be less costly overall. With renting, there is no asset to grow, but it avoids the costs of frequent home asset turnover. It is like any business making a decision. Does the gain of ownership outweigh the costs? If so, do it. If not, do not do it.

If you intend the home to be a long-term stay, then a long-term debt taken on its purchase is appropriate. You can own the asset sooner, therefore longer, by acquiring it with debt through a mortgage. This provides more time for the asset to grow in value. It also allows a lower purchase price than waiting and saving to purchase it later without a mortgage. It is very difficult to save up enough to purchase a home without a mortgage. The time spent trying to save up is time lost to the asset growth of the home.

How long should the mortgage be? You match the time of ownership properly to the intent to own the home long-term so the right answer is to match this intent with long-term debt. If the intent is to stay in a home for just a short while, the appropriate match is with short-term financing. Short-term financing is this case means renting, through the term of a lease, another form of debt.

As an asset, the home is on the lower investment portion of the Asset Reservoir of the Road Map. As debt, the mortgage is in the good side of the Debt sector above the Progress Line. Proper management will result in an asset that exceeds the debt over time. This would move the Progress Line upward over time, getting closer to your financial goal of being able to support your standard of living through sufficient wealth.

Bad debt and necessary debt are in the center of the Road Map above the Progress Line. No durable asset offsets the debt; you consume the purchase for which you used debt over time.

Necessary Debt

What is necessary debt? Necessary debt is necessary because it supports other activities required to produce income. Education and transportation are good examples. Both provide the capability and potential to get to the place of employment and bring greater skills to that employment. Getting to work allows you the ability to earn enough to pay for the cost of transportation to work. It also allows you the ability to earn more than transportation costs so you can pay the other expenses making up your standard of living. Education works in a similar manner. With the additional skill and ability comes additional income, which again allows for a higher standard of living. One could say that an automobile is an asset, but realize that it declines in value rather than increases in value. Therefore, it is important to match the debt to pay for the consumption along with the consumption (depreciation) of the automobile. This is why I categorize an auto loan as *necessary* versus *good* debt.

As with anything, necessary assets and debt come with risk. The risk of home ownership is that you may have to move sooner than planned and you suffer a loss when you sell. What is the risk for transportation? One risk is that people get more transportation than needed, or they do not properly maintain and take care of it, which means more debt than needed. What is the risk in education? If the additional ability or skill one pays to acquire is not in demand, it will not command additional income.

Bad Debt

Bad debt is debt that you still pay today for standard of living expenses (i.e. bills) acquired months ago. Clearly, this costs more than the original expense alone. Financing current consumption, where standard of living desires outstrip the capability to support that standard of living, is clearly not a good idea. Consumer debt is bad. It has the illusion of providing a better standard of living. However, having to pay for yesterday's, today's, and tomorrow's current living expenses eventually builds up to a point where it can't be maintained. It is not sustainable in the long run, and often comes to a crashing end.

Using Debt Wisely

The goal should not necessarily be debt elimination but *better use of* debt. Controlling, reducing, even eliminating *bad* consumer debt clearly should be a goal. Ensuring that necessary debt does not expand beyond reason is a reasonable goal. Keep in mind that transportation is just that: transportation. You should incur education debt only for development in areas that have long-term demand and potential. Finally, even housing debt can expand beyond reason. How? When people purchase *more home* than they really need. If there is no money left for other goal accomplishments, housing may be overdone. This is what people often refer to as being house poor. Obviously, you must pay any debt back. You should not take any debt consideration in isolation and you must consider debt along with all the other financial goals you have.

Getting dollars going towards reserves in the asset category allows you to stay out of the consumer debt trap when inevitable unforeseen expenses pop up. Tires, auto repair, refrigerator, washer, dryer, and a host of other things always pop up.

You should plan for these in the general category of reserves. You do not know what the expense will be; you just know that there will eventually be one. Otherwise, you add these extra expenses to consumer debt and the bottom just gets deeper!

Debt Is Not a Destination

Debt is a concern for many people. Debt becomes the focus of their attention. This becomes a problem because they lose sight of where they are trying to go. Becoming debt free becomes the destination. All their money goes into paying off debt. There are many problems with this. What is the real destination? They may accomplish their goal to be debt free. However, where are the assets? They gave no focus to growing the assets. The Progress Line will stay low on the Road Map. There will be no assets to push the Progress Line upward. Many argue: "When we tackle the debt, then we'll shift focus to accumulating assets." The problem is, however, that the ingredient of time is now gone. To make up for what a few dollars could have done going into assets, it now takes double, triple, or more dollars. *Time* is an extremely important ingredient. The longer you give yourself to get to a destination, the fewer of *your* dollars it takes to get there, because the first dollars compound more. See Figure 10.1. As in everything, you require balance. Balance both dollars put toward debt and dollars put toward assets. *The real answer is to control the bad debt in the first place.*

You should carefully evaluate necessary and good debt too. The bottom line is the old adage: Live within your means. You must be able to sustain any standard of living. When you use debt, what sustains the inflated standard of living you are trying to keep? Eventually it collapses and you are actually worse off. Be realistic. Be prudent. Learn to live within your means. *It takes less wealth in the end to support it.* Expand your standard of living only when you can project you are able to support it in the future through the assets you have accumulated.

CHAPTER 7

The Center of the Road Map, Unforeseen Events

Insurance provides the assets you do not have, for the needs you do have.

What if things go wrong? How do you manage the risk that something may not go according to plan? This is called *risk management* in financial planning. There are specialized modes of transportation used to cover this relatively more bumpy ground also.

I have observed in my business that risk management is one of the least understood topics in personal finance. The consequence of this is that most people are underinsured and do not realize it. Risk management confronts the risk of you losing assets or income. When someone buying auto insurance thinks of risk, typically he or she thinks of the average auto accident, for example, a dented fender. Yes, such an event hurts the budget, but it probably could be paid for. Replacing the car is the issue; or worse, a large liability resulting from a serious accident. Similarly, one could probably pay for the average hail or theft-related home insurance claim, but what about replacing the house after it burns down? People worry too much about coverage for the little claims and not enough about the bigger risks to their finances, like long-term disability. As you will see in Chapter 10, the purpose of building reserves is to be able to pay for the small deductibles and expenses, while the larger reservoir of your assets is protected with risk management tools. Risk management coverage targets the loss of a large asset or a long-term income stream.

What is Risk Management?

Risk management plays a supporting role to your overall objective of accumulating assets to support your standard of living. Risk management tools can replace lost assets, reduce debt, or both. You use the risk management tools correctly when you use them for these reasons. Lost assets obviously hurt your net worth. If a loss occurs, where would the replacement assets come from? Too much debt also hurts your net worth. If a loss occurs to your income, what is going to repay the debt? Remember that net worth equals assets minus debt.

Risk management depends on two factors: 1) probability of occurrence and, 2) cost of the loss should it occur. If something happens but is inexpensive when it does—like tearing your pants—you just *accept the loss* and replace it. If it happens a lot, you replace the pants, but you start looking at how to reduce the possibility of it happening again. This is known as *reducing* the risk.

Now, should it be likely that a loss would occur and it would be expensive, there is the tendency to *avoid* this kind of risk. An example would be racing your car. You avoid racing your car because it is highly likely a loss would occur, and it would be expensive. Alternatively, you *reduce* the risk of something expensive happening by going to the environment where everyone else is doing the same. In other words, race the car on a racetrack where everyone else has the training and experience. This reduces the risk but does not eliminate it.

Finally, for an event that has a low possibility of occurring, but would be very expensive, you can *transfer* the risk. Risk is transferred to a risk transference pool. Insurance represents risk transference pools operated by the insurance industry. They do not know who will suffer a loss. They just know that a statistically measurable portion of the pool will suffer a loss. The insurance company collects premium dollars to cover the statistical number of losses and the statistical dollar value of those losses (plus a small amount for administration and profit). If the insurer knew who would suffer the loss and how much it would be, they would refuse to write insurance for that person, and would ask that person to cover it him or herself.

Types of Risk Vehicles

There are three risk programs generally available: 1) *Government provided*—mainly Social Security; or disaster programs, 2) *Employer provided*—group insurance, and 3) *Personal insurance*—programs that you choose and manage personally. You have more control and choice with personal programs, but less with employer provided (the employer could choose to drop the program, or even drop you!), and no control over government programs.

Looking at the Road Map, where does the risk lie? At what points on the map do you see problems making the journey difficult? Let us move across the Road Map from left to right.

Figure 7.1: The WORM: Focus on Risk Management

Starting Point:
Current Cashflow
Local Area

Route of Travel:
Financial Tools

Destination:
Cashflow for
Goals and Aspirations

Work = Income

Funding

Budget

Income &
Expenses

Today's Standard
of Living Expenses

Wealth = Net Worth
(Money at Work)

Debt

Progress Line

Assets

−

+

Funding

$

Intermediate
Goals and
Aspirations

Retirement

Education

Vacations

Big
Purchases

Future Standard
of Living Expenses

Risk Management

Estate Plan

Developed by Better Financial Education 2002. Okay to reprint with this disclosure clearly visible.
Source book: Wealth Odyssey: The Essential Road Map to Reach Your Financial Goals
Modifications not authorized without permission from Better Financial Education.

Risk Management Support

Figure 7.1 WORM – Focus on Risk Management Support

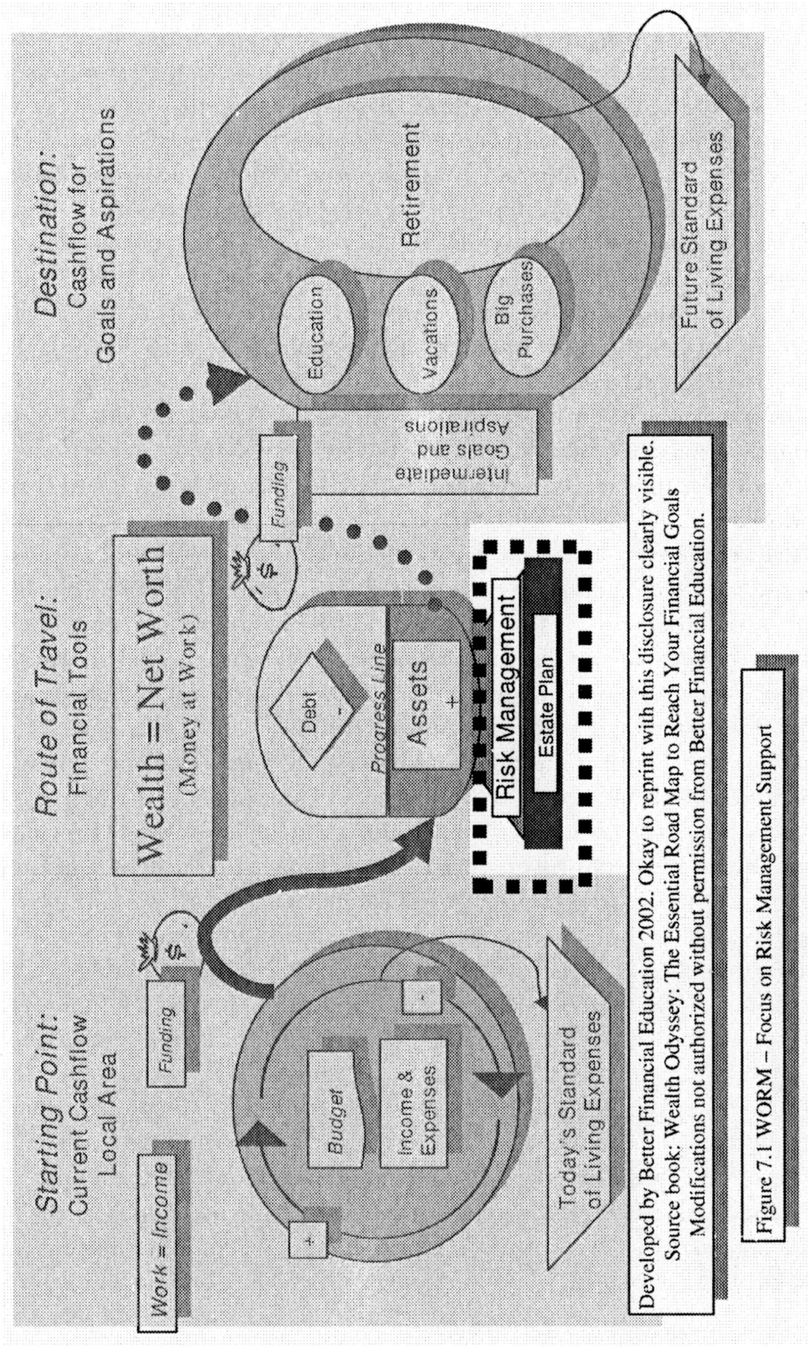

On the WORM, Risk Management is shown as a support holding your net worth in place. Without that support, unforeseen events can gobble up net worth, either by reducing or eliminating income or by consuming attained assets directly. What if you were unable to work? The risk here is the loss of income. Income is on the Left side of the Road Map. Remember that risk transference works for low probability events. Therefore, job loss is not transferable because it happens relatively frequently and is often not a randomly occurring peril; no insurer would protect against this risk. The portion of the income-loss risk that *is* transferable comes from injury or illness. The risk-transfer tool is called *disability insurance*. Obviously, if you could not work due to injury or illness, income would be in jeopardy. How would you pay your standard of living expenses this month? And what if you were out for many months? Transfer the risk. How would you be able to get to any of the future destinations you have? How do you keep the assets you already have, especially the home? Transfer the risk. Income is the source of everything else. It supports your standard of living and provides the capability to accumulate the assets to accomplish other goals you have. Transfer the risk.

What are the risks in the Center of the Road Map? The ability to preserve assets and pay debts is the most important. Paying off the debt if you are alive is part of transferring the risk we discussed above if income was lost. There is another way income can be lost: death. Income stops for this reason too. However, the debt remains and others inherit the burden to pay it. Life insurance is a risk-transfer tool that you can use to pay off debt.

Life insurance replaces the asset—it becomes the asset—that you were trying to build up to generate income later. Remember I said earlier that you needed to build wealth so work could be optional; the wealth you built would provide the income to pay standard of living expenses. Well, being dead, now you cannot build that wealth. Others around you still living have standard of living expenses today. The asset needs to become immediately available to generate the money to pay those standard of living expenses today. Where can it come from? It can come from life insurance. I use the same Wealth Rule of thumb here as I do for retirement—assets needed are assets needed, regardless of the reason. For each $5,000 per year of income needed, $100,000 of assets are needed. For example: If the family would lose $60,000 due to death of one of the wage earners, then $1,200,000 of life insurance would be needed to replace this lost income. The final element to consider here is what other goals might not be accomplished? Is there a child's education? Is there the lost capability to accumulate the retirement assets that would have accumulated? This lost accumulation of retirement assets would effect the retirement of the surviving spouse. These additional sums must be added to the lost income sum calculated above to get the total amount of income and wealth lost to the family. That becomes the amount to insure.

Another reality that puts assets, and possibly the standard of living, at risk for the spouse is frailty—the inability to look after one's basic personal needs, usually in old age (but not necessarily so—consider Christopher Reeve). Many believe their medical insurance or Medicare will take care of this, but for the most part, it will not. Medicaid may step in (MediCal in California), but assets need to be significantly spent down to qualify. Long Term Care insurance pays the additional expenses you will incur so you *do not* have to spend down accumulated assets. Why is this important? Because you need the assets for normal expenses, such as utilities and food. When you spend assets on Long Term Care needs, you spend them a lot faster. You deplete your assets sooner and you cannot pay for your basic living expenses. This area has the potential to get complex quickly. You can design coverage to do just about anything. The question is, do you pay the expenses yourself and deplete assets that you meant for other goals? Or do you transfer some or all of the risk?

I defer the discussion of what specific kinds of insurance you should get in each category to a credentialed advisor who can work out the specifics of your case. It all depends on your situation, your own concerns, goals, priorities, and your budget. As part of the Wealth Odyssey planning process, you will determine these using the advisor's help.

About Using Insurance

People tend to confuse the concept of risk management in their minds. They often ask me, "What if I never use my insurance?" The reality is that you really do not *want* to *use* insurance. You do not get insurance to use it. You get insurance so you do not have to use many more dollars to cover a loss. The ideal circumstance is never to make a claim. Really, the fundamental value of insurance is as a risk transfer tool to protect assets and income so that you can accomplish your goals and destinations—anyway—in the event of unforeseen events. So stop wondering about not having to use it. The benefit of insurance is that *if* you do have to use it, it protects other assets from depletion. Risk management, in short, supports the assets in the Road Map by transferring the risk to those assets for pennies on the dollar. You spend relatively little to keep the asset dollars safe from the larger expense of loss if something adverse happens.

CHAPTER 8

The Center of the Road Map, Success

What if everything goes right? You have the wealth to support your standard of living expenses and get to the other destinations for which you have set out. Congratulations! However, having money and stuff also brings with it a completely new set of questions. These questions begin to crop up even if we have not arrived at our destinations yet. The fact that we have stuff now becomes a problem. We now must begin to think about *estate planning*. And that conjures up all kinds of new thoughts for discussion. Estate planning is a multi-level topic; there is a basic level of planning that applies to most of us, and for many there is a more advanced level. Estate planning, on the WORM, is another foundation created to support the Net Worth base, and specifically the Asset Reservoir (see Figure 7.1). Estate planning supports the net worth base by reducing expenses related to transferring assets to others.

Basic Estate Planning

You have stuff. Questions arise about what to do with this stuff, essentially boiling down to: *Who, what, when, where, why, and how?* Who gets it? What do they get? When do they get it? Where is it? Why should they get it? In addition, how do they get it? Before you even start talking to anyone about planning, you need to have these questions answered in your own mind. Forget about estate taxes for the moment. That subject comes up in advanced estate planning. When you have *lots* of stuff, then things get more complicated. An experienced estate-planning attorney familiar with these advanced tax and estate issues would then be required.

The assets successfully accumulated now need to be distributed. You would rather this distribution be according to your specific wishes rather than state legal guidelines. Basic estate planning supports your assets through helping to ensure the distribution and use of those assets according to your specific wishes. Proper planning also helps preserve your assets according to your wishes.

The next phase in thinking regards your capacity to manage your stuff while you are still alive. What happens if you become incapacitated and can no longer manage your financial affairs? You need to answer the same questions. Do the answers change if you are still alive? It is okay, because the answers may change. What you want to happen while alive may be different from what you want after you depart. It is your stuff and your goals. *Conservatorship* addresses how others manage your assets when you are still here in body, but not here in mind, so to speak. For whatever reason, you are not able to address your financial issues yourself, so you should choose and appoint others, through *living trusts, durable power of attorney,* and similar tools, to take over. Now, after you have your basic estate planning desires in mind, you can start talking with an attorney to draw up the documents that make your wishes known and carry them out. Should you have a Will and/or a Living Trust? Basically, a Will works when you are gone-gone. A Living Trust does the same, but it also works when you are here-gone (incapacitated for some reason). You should not talk with just any attorney. You should talk with an attorney with a specialty is estate planning. You should get documents specific to your wishes and goals rather than generic documents.

Advanced Estate Planning

Advanced estate planning brings in the complexities of federal gift and estate taxes on assets passed to others. Some states also apply inheritance taxes. There may also be income tax issues on some of the property, such as retirement accounts. Advanced estate-planning works ahead of time to determine what taxes may apply and what strategies you may use to reduce these taxes. To address this topic is beyond the scope of this book. Advanced estate planning becomes an issue when the value of the total estate exceeds a couple of million dollars. It is hard to put an exact figure today on this value, as the tax code in this area is changing. The best course of action is to consult a knowledgeable advanced estate tax attorney who is aware of the tax implications of various planning strategies. However, whether or not your asset base qualifies for the advanced treatment, do not forget to cover basic estate planning—that applies to everyone.

Where Retirement Planning and Estate Planning Intersect

One might think, on the surface, that Retirement Planning—supporting yourself financially when alive—is unrelated to Estate Planning, which comes into play primarily at death. However, in practice, the designation of beneficiaries is one of the most overlooked areas in retirement planning. Proper beneficiary designations are part of any basic estate plan. All retirement plans also need to have both primary and contingent beneficiaries listed. Without proper designations, the IRS and/or state law may decide for you. It is important to understand that those provisions may not be what you want, and may not accomplish what you think you are accomplishing. The minimum required distribution rules of retirement plans, tax and inheritance laws, trusts, and probate laws all have a complex interaction for your retirement plans that are sufficient in size to support you as a retiree. Failure to plan properly can cause assets to go to the wrong beneficiary, and in addition may trigger large tax bills, both for income *and* estate tax. This topic is important, and professional estate planning help is valuable. Further reading is available: *Life and Death Planning for Retirement Benefits* and *The 100 Best and Worst Planning Ideas for Your Client's Retirement Benefits*, both by Natalie Choate. You can find these references and other information related to this topic at www.ataxplan.com.

Part III

Your Journey Begins

CHAPTER 9

Planning Your Wealth Odyssey

We need to learn to set our course by the stars, not by the lights of every passing ship.

—Omar Bradley

The purpose of planning any trip is to ensure you have enough money for the trip and you know how to get to each destination. You also know what you are going to do when you get there. You look at what there is to do of interest to you, and you budget for it. You use different strategies to decide where to stay and how to move about. Often you plan and imagine the trip one way only to find that once on the trip things are different. You adapt along the way.

The planning portion of your financial journey happens in much the same way. The difference is that you are less familiar with the different methods of transportation and are very unfamiliar with the destinations. The purpose of strategy is to smooth out the unknowns, many of which are brought on by the uncertainty in the economy and financial markets. When used properly, you build the Assets part of the Road Map to accomplish your goals. This helps get you to your destinations. If your goals do not change, then the strategy does not change either. Sure, there will be storms along the way. Proper use of a strategy allows you to ride out those storms.

In today's investing world, there are many *now* suggestions. What these now suggestions lack is anything to do with where you are right now, or your destination, or any of your chosen strategies. These now suggestions often have more to do with who is suggesting them than with you, i.e. more to do with *their* reasons than yours. Work with a credentialed advisor who is interested in *your* reasons.

Measuring Progress on Your Journey

For a trip, you measure distance in miles, not in yards or feet. Why? Because miles describes the distance in terms that we better understand. Yet, in accumulating wealth, people want to measure in terms of just one metric, *interest*. That is like measuring a road trip in yards. The proper measurement is in terms of *total return*. This is a long-term measurement, appropriate for goals further away in time. The number ends with a percent sign—just like interest—but how the number is derived is different. Interest implies constant increases in value with no declines. Total return expresses the return with all things considered—income, plus growth or decline in value over the long haul. For the Wealth Odyssey, you need to think in terms of miles. The destination is farther away. Miles provides more information than yards. Begin to think of your more distant goals in terms of total return. You address near-term goals through assets that deliver interest. You address long-term goals through assets delivering *total return*.

Time-weighted returns tell you what the return is over the period in question. That takes into account whether dollars were added at a good time or poor time—that is, during strong, expensive markets or during weak, relatively cheap markets. Today's investors tend to measure their return in dollar-weighted returns, the change in value now compared to what was originally invested. This ignores *when* those dollars went in and *how much* the amount invested differed each time. To get an actual return, the investor needs to calculate the return on each payment individually, adding and averaging these returns appropriately. For example, let us invest $100,000 initially for six months and receive a return of *negative* 10 percent (value now $90,000). At the end of that first six months, we invest $500,000 and receive a 5 percent return on the new base of $590,000. The ending value is $619,500, an increase of $19,500. But the total return is a negative 5.5 percent. That is correct, a negative total return. Why? When the returns were negative, the investor did not have a lot of money invested so the investor lost a modest $10,000. When the returns were positive, the investor had a lot more invested so a small gain (5 percent) resulted in a larger dollar gain, $29,500. This is the error of thinking in terms of dollars and not in terms of returns. Geometric return evaluates the investment, not the timing of the cash into the investment.

Time-weighted returns allow you to compare your progress with that of others. Time-weighted rate of return computes the holding period return, and geometrically averages the returns of multiple holding periods, resulting in a *geometric* average return. Dollar-weighted returns, or simple averages, only tell you *your own* results. You cannot use your dollar-weighted returns to compare yourself to anyone else, or to the performance of markets, because the timing of their investments—and thus their success—is likely to be different from yours, even if they hold the same investments. A time-weighted return with geometric averaging forms a more realistic basis for judging performance and comparing to others. The math for this calculation is beyond the scope of this book but you can find examples in *Value Investing for Dummies*, Wiley 2001. You can find a good discussion of the use and misuse of returns as well in *A Mathematician Plays the Stock Market* (Appendix E). You can read a more thorough treatment including software in *Investments, an Introduction* (Appendix E).

All detail aside, the main point: *You are better off comparing your performance against yourself,* against your own goals, rather than against others. Your benchmark should be how you are doing towards your specific goals. You are not interested in knowing whether you are beating a generic benchmark, such as the S&P 500 Index, because that benchmark does not relate to your goal! That benchmark does not know how fast you should be going. You could be beating an external benchmark handily with some money. However, if that sum of money is not going to be enough for your goal, what have you accomplished? Your own benchmark should be desired progress along the way to your own goal. If you are behind achieving your own goal, this tells you that you need to do something to catch up (change the goal, or add more money, etc.). Your own Progress Line from your own Road Map is more informative than any generic benchmark could be. Calculate your own Progress Line with your own SOIL using the Wealth Rule.

The Importance of Asset Allocation

You have often heard that asset allocation and diversification is important. Conventional wisdom and thinking changes what asset is favored or disfavored over time. Rather than try to guess which asset it will be, the prudent investor diversifies. Nobody can know what will be, only what was. Behavioral economists have recently examined our financial behavior. They have found that people's mental accounting often has them do something contrary to thinking that is more rational. For example, people think of gains in terms of percentages, but losses in terms of dollars. Dollars are more real to us so we feel losses worse than gains. These feelings cause us to do things when we should not be doing them. Elements of complexity science and chaos theory enter the discussion of the many financial markets, which we will discuss later in stochastic modeling. Many factors enter into the study about why markets fluctuate in value and how to model that fluctuation and contend with it emotionally.

Group psychology becomes a factor as everybody tries to figure out what everybody else will do in the markets. Things constantly change, regardless of the market in question. While things change, you search for the market expectations that other people will adopt. Simultaneously, they are searching for market expectations you will adopt. Expectations form conventional thinking to deal with this problem of everybody trying to figure out what everybody else will do. Conventional thinking is difficult to change. It takes a jolt to create different, unconventional, new thinking. Then the search-for-expectations cycle begins again. It is dizzying to try to keep up with markets with all these forces at work, which is why they seem confusing to many.

For a clarifying analogy, behavioral finance suggests that money is like a school of fish. At any given moment, we know where the school is. We are not sure where it might be tomorrow. The school runs where the food is, or where the perceived danger is not. Money runs where returns are now, or where the perceived risk is less. Money changes directions, just like a school of fish, without notice and upon imperceptible changes in the environment. Rather than try to guess where the school of fish is going to be each day, you should instead determine where the fishing holes are. Where do the fish always seem to hang out? If they are not here, then where else do they go? Rather than chase the fish and miss them, why not just drop nets in all the fishing holes? Some are going to come up dry because no fish are there that day. Others are going to produce fish. Put a net in all the fishing holes and you will get fish. It is the same with money. People chase where the money was yesterday. If there are no returns, they come up empty for the day (a loss). Asset allocation and diversification cover all the areas money tends to go. This analogy shows how asset allocation and diversification help smooth out the mob mentality.

Asset allocation means having many baskets for your assets, and diversification means placing many different eggs in each of those baskets. The baskets and eggs need to be dissimilar. Not all stock is similar, nor are all bonds, and cash is also different. Less liquid choices include real estate and other tangible assets (assets that are real and can be touched versus paper assets, like collectibles). The purpose here is to ensure you are not doing the opposite—concentrating your assets. How does concentrating hurt? Ask anyone about concentrating in technology in 1999 and ignoring other parts of the economy. How did this happen? Because people noticed how rapidly investments in technology went up. Short-term performance started to become the goal, displacing the real goal, *your* goal. Your goal is to arrive at your financial destination. This is the reason you are accumulating assets. The goal is not simply to make money. Rather, the goal should be to build wealth to support your unique standard of living.

Core and Explore Investing

Asset allocation and diversification requires discipline. You should invest the *core* base of assets in a disciplined manner. If you are tempted to chase a little performance, recognize it and put a small amount in the *explore* category. Do not be tempted to move the serious core over to explore just because explore is doing fantastic. History suggests that in time that will change. The real discipline is to take from explore when it is doing well and move the profits back to the staid and boring serious core.

Dollar Cost Averaging

Dollar cost averaging works well as a strategy during your accumulation years. One bases this strategy on the concept of adding dollars when you have them, and adding more dollars consistently over time, typically monthly since this is when most people get additional money. Properly applied, it buys a portfolio of stock, usually in the form of mutual funds. This is because there is risk that any individual stock could go down and continue going down, even to zero, so putting more in would mean losing more. A mutual fund reduces the risk of total loss because it is unlikely all of a fund's holdings would go to zero simultaneously. This, however, does not fully eliminate risk. It does not. The objective is to accumulate shares. Your money buys more shares when prices are lower, so you have more shares to go up in value when prices go up. It also automatically buys fewer shares when prices are higher, so you have fewer shares to go down in relative value. Over the long run—and this is a long-term accumulation strategy—the shares you bought when lowest will go up the most in value. When investing lump sums, you invest when you have the money. You should prudently invest the money as a lump sum now because in the long term now is historically the lowest price relative to when you take the money out. This is hard to do for some people, so investing half now and dollar cost averaging the other half, is an example of a compromise strategy serving to comfort many people.

Mutual Funds

Many investors feel there is some magic to investing in specific individual companies. The historical record shows that individual stocks can lose money for the average investor, while investing in the overall market has historically paid off. Should you do it yourself? Alternatively, do you hire a professional? You can find professional money managers through retail mutual funds, institutional asset class funds, or separately managed accounts. A tour guide would definitely be helpful in defining and assisting you on your journey.

There are many different ways to classify professionally managed investments. One way is to define their target audience: How much in assets you have determines what kind of management structure you use. One could divide funds into retail funds and institutional asset class funds. *Retail mutual funds* are for those who have less than six figures (less than $100,000) to invest. *Institutional asset class funds* are for those with more than six figures (more than $100,000) and *separately managed accounts* are for those with more than seven figures (more than $1,000,000). Funds tend to invest in just one main asset class, so you would need multiple funds to provide the diversification you need to have an effective asset allocation strategy.

Stochastic Modeling

Be conscious of the faults in trying to use linear, deterministic modeling to determine or project the results of your efforts. What is linear modeling? Most software takes the average return plugged in and multiplies that same input repeatedly to get the result. Markets do not produce same returns year after year. Nevertheless, these models calculate a single answer. It will be mathematically correct but unlikely to be the amount you realize when you actually arrive in the future. Why? Because markets deviate in real life. Statistics provides a measure known as *standard deviation*, measuring fluctuations in returns around a norm that occurs over the years. Deterministic calculations just plugging in a single average growth-rate figure ignore the fact that markets do not act this way. Financial markets do not have constant returns without fluctuations. Not even interest rates stay the same.

In the past, financial planners worked hard to identify investor risk tolerance and would analyze asset allocation for risk and return with this tolerance in mind. Their resulting projections assumed that no matter how much or little risk, it would disappear when it comes to calculating future values. This is because none of the calculations considered the fact that future returns change; they ignored standard deviation. As mentioned above, the timing of those variations is important. We do not know when different returns will occur, nor do we know what the return will be when we receive it. This is where *stochastic modeling* comes in.

Stochastic modeling determines not only an amount of return from an investment but also the *probability* of receiving that amount at different time intervals. It simulates the markets up and downs. Nobody knows the future, but market simulation can get you one-step closer than blindly ignoring market ups and downs. The purpose is to generate an idea of feasibility and likelihood of certain outcomes. Will what you are trying to do with your investments work? Does it depend on an improbable outcome, and will modifications be necessary? You want to modify your strategy before you start because you want to avoid as many surprises as possible.

You still need to monitor things as you go, because it is difficult to know for sure on which simulated track you are. In addition, you can be switching simulated tracks as you go through time. In other words, just because things are going well, you cannot assume they always will. The other unknown is the probability of your longevity. To what age are you going to live? Estimating a probability of that, along with probabilities of accumulation amounts, gets your thinking and discussion going in the proper direction. The point is that there is no one right answer, but a range of probable answers. Arguing about what those probable answers might be is good for academic refinement, but does not help you get closer to your goal. Knowing the range of probabilities *does* help you determine how you are doing towards your unique goals and helps you benchmark yourself on your own Progress Line.

The purpose of modeling is to determine the feasibility of a plan. It does not predict anything. You still do not know the future. Are you on track for the goal? Does the model show that you are on a bad track or good track? Maybe some combination thereof that is always changing. Remember, you do not know the future until it becomes the past! Modeling provides you with some idea of feasibility. Modeling provides some parameters of likely success. Modeling shows where the stress points might lie. Monitoring these parameters becomes most important, rather than reacting to daily and even hourly noise. This is like adjusting the old TV antenna to reduce the snow. You looked through the snow at the picture to improve the picture. You did not look at the snow itself.

Generic Benchmarks

Generic benchmarks tell you what a financial market segment did, but not what *you* did. They also do not tell you what is going to happen. What you need is a *Goal Index* or *Family Index* that tells you how you are progressing towards your goal. That is what probabilistic modeling does. The Dow Jones Industrial Average, NASDAQ Composite, S&P 500, Wilshire 5000, and so forth are like airplane gauges. If you have seen the cockpit of an airplane, have you noticed all the gauges and dials? The bigger the plane, the more gauges there are because there are more factors to measure. And no one gauge tells the full story. The pilot needs to interpret them all. All those benchmark-investing figures thrown at you are similar to the airplane gauges. They do not tell you in what to invest or what will happen. They tell you what has already happened. A goal index developed through probabilistic methods tells what is relevant because it measures progress to your own destination. It is specific to you. It is the navigational beacon that correspondes to your own personal goals. Your Progress Line can tell you how far you have come towards that electronic beacon. Set your overall destination. Determine the strategies you will use. Do not change the strategy because the weather has changed. Change the strategy when you are approaching the destination.

Scenic Side Trip 9.1: The Great Modeling Debate

There is a debate occurring in the financial services business among the more mathematical thinkers. The debate is a good thing, and the result of its supporting research and analysis is a good thing. What it brings to the discussion between you and a credentialed advisor is a good thing. However, to think that one can precisely determine what *will* happen is not possible, even with the most advanced mathematical models. All that one can say is what *might* happen. That implies possibility and probability, which is the topic of the great debate. The research is on how to refine the determination of the correct answer.

What is the problem? The problem is in the deterministic and probabilistic calculations that tell how much you need to meet a financial goal. Deterministic calculations are what we all learned about in school. Given a starting value, a rate of return, additional money added, and the time-period, you can calculate a single resulting number—one number that is it—mathematically precise and correct. That is what electronic calculators and computer software do. They determine the number, hence, the name deterministic. However, what if the rate of return changes each year? The returns you find in the markets vary. The solution to this in the past was to plug in a different single return number, maybe be more conservative. The same goes for number of dollars added, that could change too. All those deterministic calculations ignore the questions: What is the *chance* of things happening that one single way? What if *all* the variables were to change all at the same time?

Stochastic modeling was designed to resolve probability mainly by plugging in random returns. This modeling can calculate the result of constantly changing returns. However, who says the markets will generate returns in a specific *order*? Yes, the order of returns matters, too. The answer is to model multiple variations of the returns over the same time period to generate a range of probabilities of results. Sounds good so far.

Nevertheless, all sides of the argument still ignore the underlying issue—what *will* happen? Nobody knows! Absolutely nobody! This does not mean the exercise is useless. Again, the utility comes from recognizing what results and their probability could be under a multitude of different circumstances. Each of these possibilities would have an impact on what you do. However, you still cannot know this in advance! Modifying what you do as time goes on is still a necessity. Just because it works in the model does not mean you set it up on autopilot and forget about it!

In light of this, asset allocation and diversification are extremely important. You don't make wholesale changes to everything; you do make changes on the margin, along the edges, so to speak, based on what is currently happening and how you feel about what is happening. Again, it is not switching from what was hot to the next thing that is hot. That is just chasing returns and is often precisely what you should not do. What you must do is to look hard at things, especially if you are taking distributions from your portfolio and have no capability of replacing the assets in the future, for example in retirement.

There is now better understanding and realization that simple and precise calculations mask many issues. The debate and continuing research and analysis is good to refine those shortfalls. It is important to look at the results of higher-level thought and calculations to get a better grasp of all the issues, and to set up your portfolio based on those issues. However, it is also important to recognize that ongoing monitoring and adjustments are still required once what was unknown now becomes known.

It would be good to read the Scenic Side Trip discussion on what money can do during withdrawal phase in Chapter 12 (SST 12.1). These are intertwined topics.

CHAPTER 10

Potholes and Headwinds

The measure of success is not whether you have a tough problem to deal with, but whether it is the same problem that you had last year.

—John Foster Dulles

In this chapter, we will examine some of the things that can go wrong, or simply create headwinds, impeding progress on your Wealth Odyssey. Some of these, like procrastination, are controllable, while others, like inflation, are not. As manager of your own Wealth Odyssey, you need to be aware of these issues, and do what you can to change them or mitigate their effects.

Procrastination

Procrastination hurts asset growth, growth in the primary component of net worth. Procrastination retards growth. Thus, the cost of procrastination is what it takes to make up for lost time. It is the first—repeating—first dollars invested that grow the most. Why? Those first dollars have had the most time to grow and the most time to *compound*. By not giving assets time to grow, that growth is stunted. The effects of compounding are more pronounced when more time is allowed for the growth. By reducing time through procrastination, the back end part of the exponential compounding curve is lost. Figure 10.1 shows how the effect of procrastination is not the loss of the small amount of savings in the initial years (Area A), but rather the much larger shortfall that occurs down the road (Area B). Indeed, the penalty for procrastination is high.

Figure 10.1: The Effect of Delayed Savings

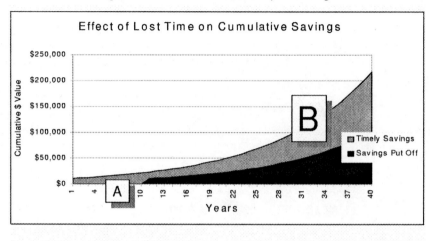

Figure 10.1 The Effect of Delayed Savings

Inflation

Inflation is the slow and insidious increase in the dollar costs of goods and services. If inflation isn't factored into your plans, you run the risk that your eventual Net Worth will not cover your future expenses. People do not think in terms of what Net Worth needs to pay for in the future. If you are not working, in other words, are retired, where is the money going to come from to buy groceries and pay the phone, cable, and other utility bills? Out of a Net Worth that was projected based on your cost of living at the time of the projection, not necessarily that of the future. Is your phone bill (cell or otherwise) more today than it was before? That is inflation. Those increased expenses in the future put pressure on your Net Worth to support those increased costs. Put another way, it acts as a headwind, slightly reducing the value of your saved dollars as you move forward in time, and requiring yet a few more dollars to be set aside.

Unforeseen Events

The best-laid plans are often undermined by unforeseen events or unforeseen expenditures. For example: loss of home, loss of job, income loss from an injury or illness that prevents working, liabilities from a home or auto accident, or the additional expenses of care if you become frail in old age. All of these force either or both asset shrinkage and debt increases. These will force a reduction in the standard of living you have today and most likely—unless covered in your financial plans—for the future. This is the reason for insurance, a risk management tool that transfers the risk to a pool sharing the risk. The statistical nature of the risk game comes into play here. For a few known dollars paid upfront as premium, you transfer your large and unknown risk to others in the insurance pool. Should you be the *statistical one* to suffer the loss, then the few dollars collected from each of the many add up to the large sum you need to overcome the financial loss.

Figure 10.2: Types of Risk and Risk Management Tools

Risk and Risk Management		
	RISK	**RISK MANAGEMENT SOLUTION**
INCOME RISK	•Loss of Job	•Asset Reserve
	•Loss of Life	•Life Insurance
	•Disability (Loss of Income)	•Asset Reserves (for waiting periods) •Social Security (Disability/Retirement) •Disability Insurance
ASSET RISK	•Property Damage	•Asset Reserves (for deductibles) •Property/Casualty Insurance (auto,homeowners etc)
	•Frailty	•Asset Reserves (for waiting periods) •Long Term Care Insurance
	•Living Too Long	•Social Security/Pension •Immediate Annuities

Figure 10.2 Types of Risk and Risk Management Tools

Income Reduction from Injury or Illness

Does your income continue if you cannot work due to injury or illness? Some employers provide for sick days. Beyond these days, there may be some short-term disability income coverage, through Workers Compensation or other mandated programs. Beyond the short term, there may be disability income coverage, perhaps provided by mandatory state disability funds, that continues for a fixed number of years. There is also a disability provision within Social Security, but it takes a very serious disability to qualify. Bottom line: Do not get complacent here. Even if your employer supplies disability insurance and pays the premiums when you receive the benefit, it will be taxable income. Taxes naturally reduce your take-home portion of the benefit. However, be aware that the benefit is reduced to begin with, usually it is 50 to 75 percent of your original salary! It is not likely that this will pay your full household budget. You can fill in the gaps with your own purchased personal disability income insurance. When *you* pay the premium (with after-tax dollars), you receive the benefit dollars in full, free of income tax. There are many more potholes: income reduction from job loss; a sick child or other medical expenses; increased taxes, stock market dips, pension plan failures, living too long, etc. For some of these there is little that can be done beforehand and they require adaptation once they become reality. However, reserves is a good starting point and one area I see very little of among clients and people I teach in my class.

Integrating Reserves with Insurance Planning

One key principle of insurance: the less you tap the insurance bucket for benefits, the lower the premiums become. Higher deductibles or longer waiting periods means you pay out of pocket first, then tap the insurance for benefits exceeding the amount of the deductible. People often see using their dollars first as a problem, so they get low deductibles or short waiting periods, which costs much more. If you have reserves, you can raise your deductibles and waiting periods and use those reserves to pay for those first dollars required. The resulting decrease in premiums means you have freed up dollars for other goals, including building reserves. Make those freed up dollars first fund those goals automatically.

Living Too Long

Like any trip that goes on too long, living too long can be a serious pothole for your Wealth Odyssey! There is a triad of solution sources: government programs, employer programs, and personally established programs. To address the problem of living too long, Social Security is a government safety net for those qualified and eligible to participate. The second leg of the triad may come from an employer in the form of a Defined Benefit pension plan, paying pensions as long as a retiree lives. Such programs also have a private safety net through the Pension Benefit Guarantee Corporation (PBGC); however, the retiree's pension benefit may be reduced if the company plan needs to be rescued through this program (which is not government backed). The third leg of the triad is through personal retirement savings established either through an employer or individually. Of course, if either of the other two legs of the triad does not apply, then you have to solve the whole problem through personal savings.

You could convert some of the assets you save personally in your Asset Reservoir to a guaranteed income for life through an immediate annuity from an insurance company. When *annuitized* these annuities set up payments guaranteed for *as long as you live* from the point they begin. They differ from standard annuities designed to accumulate tax-deferred assets. Of course, the strength of the insurance company is important as well—you want to be sure the insurance company lasts longer than you do! The discussion of annuities is beyond the scope of this book and companies are constantly updating annuities to address the challenges of providing various kinds of guarantees.

Frailty

Frailty for purposes of our discussion is not being able to care fully for yourself. Since 1996, the government has placed the cost of this type of care on the individual through personally acquired Long Term Care (LTC) insurance. This insurance can pay for either in-home care or care services across a spectrum of community-provided care situations up to and including the nursing home. The fundamental issue: No one knows *if* he or she will need the care. If you know that you need it, then you will not qualify for the insurance. This is no different from any other insurance; if your house burns down, it is too late to get insurance. By not buying LTC insurance you put your retirement assets at risk. Remember, the assets in the Asset Reservoir are there to provide for your SOIL. Frailty expenses are over and above the SOIL needs considered by most people. This means that the additional withdrawals will empty your Asset Reservoir faster and you will run out of money too soon. At that point you may qualify for the government provided program through Medicaid (MediCal in California) but you would become impoverished in so doing—not the desired end result of good financial planning.

Scenic Side Trip 10.1: When Do You Want to Run Out of Money?

When do you want to run out of money? That seems like an unusual question. Let us think about that for a moment. We certainly do not want to run out of money when we are still alive and retired, do we? Once retired, where is the money to buy life's necessities going to come from if we do indeed run out of wealth? Once we are gone, it does not matter. However, when will that be? Prudent planning would dictate that you manage your wealth so you will not run out. You can see where the idea of trying to protect principal is appealing. It comes from this very problem. You want to protect the principal and live off its income. However, there is another way…

Responding to Economic Cycles: The Total Return Approach

What is total return? How is total return different from the idea people typically have about the need to keep principal constant so that they can live off the interest? Protecting principal means taking on less risk and reducing interest, or earnings. Living off the interest may sound good, however, it has the insidious effect of making people too conservative when the economy and markets are doing well, and too aggressive when the economy and markets are doing poorly. Total return, on the other hand, looks at both earnings and value. As long as one controls how much is taken from his or her portfolio overall, there is always something there for later.

Let me explain a bit more. When the economy is doing well, the Federal Reserve gets worried about it overheating, and interest rates rise as the Fed moves to prevent the inflation that could result. So, when times are good, interest rates are higher, which should provide the income many are looking for. However, many people do not feel the need to stretch their risk any further if they have the income they need. They tend to be happy with what they have and remain more conservative, just harvesting the interest from their investments. Of course, there are those who have enough income and *still* reach for more yield. In other words, they want still higher interest rates, which call for more risk. When things go well for a longer stretch, a couple of years, people begin to count on this good fortune and expand their Standard of Individual Living (expenses). People spend more. To do this from a portfolio, they *reach for more yield* (income) to support these increased expenditures. It is insidious because it means taking more risk; the good times are not long lasting. When things turn bad, they are caught off guard.

When the economy is doing poorly, the Fed does the opposite. Interest rates fall as the Fed works to keep interest and capital costs low, helping to stimulate the economy. With low interest rates, even those people who were happy with status-quo interest payments find that lower rates mean lower income. Their reaction is to search for higher interest rates to keep up with expenses. That means taking on higher risk. They are *chasing yield* and taking on more risk than they should in an environment where the economy is doing poorly.

By managing your portfolio for total return, on the other hand, you smooth out the peaks and valleys. When Net Worth is increasing, it can support a higher distribution. The question becomes: Why spend it? Move the excess value to reserves to protect it from the inevitable decline in value. Remember that everything cycles up and down in value. Tap this asset reserve when the cyclic decline does come to provide the money you need while the main portfolio recovers its value. By managing just one component of the portfolio, you expose yourself to the peaks and valleys of that component. The result? Income streams rise and fall uncontrollably.

CHAPTER 11

Using the Road Map to Achieve Your Goals and Destinations

There is more to life than increasing its speed.
—Mohandas Gandhi

There is more to life than increasing its greed.
—Affluenza
(De Graaf, Wann, Naylor, 2002)

As we saw in Chapter 3, military planning provides a useful analogy for planning your Wealth Odyssey. There are lots of targets but limited resources. This is the same issue you have with money. Many things you want to do, but limited resources. Military planning provides a good example of how to break down this dilemma. First, there is the overall objective. Within the objective, various *campaigns* address sub-objectives. Then, *phases* address the timing of when to address each sub-objective. *Contingency planning* addresses the question of what if things go wrong, or not according to plan. Finally, the plan looks at what to do if things go right.

The Wealth Odyssey—Military Style

With this in mind, what is your overall objective for your Wealth Odyssey? Answer: to increase Net Worth. What are your campaigns? Answer: your different goals and the priority for each goal. What are the phases? Answer: the timing of the dollars for those goals. Note here that the priority may go to the last campaign, but there may be many phases between now and then. Why is this important? Because your resources go to the high priority goals, not your goal that arrives soonest! Contingency plans? Risk management is for those things that

96

could go wrong. What if you lose your job? What if there is injury, illness, or death? What assets are at risk of loss? From where would that risk of loss come? The end game? Now you have succeeded. What happens now? Answer: estate planning. There are many questions to answer.

You have lots of possible destinations or goals. What is your overall objective? What are your primary destinations? What is the priority of all these destinations? Note that in real life, the timing of certain goals does not necessarily reflect the priority of a goal. Some lower priority goals may happen first just because of the timing. Lower priority just means that you do not fund them completely. You have limited resources—money and assets.

What are the different goals at different times? These are the stops along the way, destinations on the way to the main destination. Transfer the risk. When you get to your final destination—retirement for most people—what do you do with the success? How do you manage the assets now? Do you manage your assets differently than while accumulating them? What if things go wrong, who gets them in the end? Basic estate planning that addresses each of the questions: who, what, why, when, where and how? If taxes become an issue, then you need advanced estate planning.

Many people lose sight of the real goal. They spend all their time concentrating on the Left side of the Road Map, spending everything they make, and finding ways to make ends meet. Worse, they divert dollars into debt to create the illusion of a higher standard of living. This impedes the progress to cross the Road Map to reach the Right side. Others spend all their time wandering in the middle of the Road Map experimenting with different modes of transportation, i.e., experimenting with what they should invest in now. The real focus must first be on the destination. Most do not know where they are trying to go. They do not even know where *there* is! Once you know, what your destination is—what your goal is—then how to get there becomes more apparent. You do not change modes of transportation during a storm. Nor should you change an appropriate mode of investing during a market storm. You determine this change by how distant in time the goal is. It is easy to substitute a pseudo destination, e.g., simply making money, if you lack a destination. This often leads to aimless wandering without getting anywhere.

Don't Let the Salespeople Decide

Do not let the financial sales process determine your destination. Do not let the sales process determine what your goals are. *You* determine your goals. Ask help to get there and there only.

Do not let a sales process put you on a detour. Clearly understand how the different modes of transportation can get you to your destination. When you study materials and read other books, look at them from the perspective: "How does it fit into my Road Map?" Does it build wealth in a way you can use it to get to your destination? Does it support that wealth in case something goes wrong? There are no right answers. Only those right for you. Why? Because other people have their own origins and destinations. They have the same Road Map you do, but they are not going to the same place you are. It is like saying I am going to New York. There are still a lot of different places in New York. I am going to retirement. There are many different kinds of retirement.

Revisiting the Right Side

This chapter re-examines and gives more detail about the Right side of the Road Map. What are your goals? How do you answer this question, which is so broad? In personal finance, it comes down to condensing your many goals into a critical few so that resources can be efficiently applied to accomplish them. It comes down to the question: What is your overall objective? What is it that you want to accomplish above everything else? What are your concerns? Brainstorm here. Just jot ideas down as they occur to you. Do not leave anything out at this point. Keep brainstorming. Then decide, what are the priorities of these concerns you have written down? Change these concerns into goals or a group of goals. Which goal has the highest priority, then the next and the next? This tells you where to focus your resources. It also tells you where you come up short. Do you need to reorder your priorities once you realize where you are short?

More about Budgeting

How do you apply resources to your goals? Do you budget? Budgeting has taken on a life of its own and I believe it has lost its original intent. What is the purpose of budgeting? Is it to be sure you spent money appropriately? No. Budgeting should not be about self-denial; avoiding this or that so you can use the money for something else. Budgeting starts at the wrong place. Today it means determining where your money has gone. That is the wrong focus. *You need to determine where you want the money to go.* Then make it go there! Budgeting is a planning process. A primary result of budgeting is making dollars go automatically to build Net Worth to achieve the goals you have determined. Then you can spend what is left. *You do not need to keep track of today's expenses as long as you have taken care of tomorrows already.*

Really, contrary to what many think, this mode of operation *puts you first*. It is the opposite of consumerism, which in a way that *puts them first*. What does this mean? Marketers and others who expect to benefit encourage you to spend on them first and then on you. If you automatically put dollars into the modes of transportation that take you to your goals, then these dollars go to you first. You spend the dollars that remain on them. This manner of budgeting also makes it a more positive experience, not a what-do-I-have-to-give-up negative experience. Plan—and budget—with the end in mind.

Putting Purpose on the Road Map

Purpose is what you deeply care about; it is larger than goals. Purpose is what is important to you and includes aspirations, not just basic needs. At the same time, *concerns* are anything that may hinder, or impede, as a roadblock, the attainment of purpose. In order to achieve what you deeply care about, you need to address these concerns. *Goals* address your concerns, clearing them out of the way, so that you can achieve your purpose.

For example, your *purpose* might be to take care of your family such that they have every opportunity to succeed on their own. Your *concerns* might be what if something happens before you can help them. Another concern is being able to save enough for retirement. Some goals that you might set with these concerns in mind are: education funding to help the children; saving for your own retirement; ensuring that income continues in case of injury or illness; buying life insurance so all the goals are funded if you don't have enough time to fund them while working; and being sure the house is safe and protected to continue to provide shelter and a home. The final step is to prioritize each of these so that you can take the last step and allocate resources to the highest priority on down, until resources run out. There is no *right answer* because priorities are up to each individual.

Left, Right—Or Right, Left?

You *live* life moving from the present into the future. You cannot stop the clock. You *plan* life by determining your preferred future and try to ensure the resources are there when you arrive. Therefore, I suggest you use the Road Map from right to left with a clear purpose illuminating what you are trying to do while you plan. With this in mind, budgeting has a clear meaning. There are many possible destinations, but how do we get to each one? For example, do you have thoughts of retirement? Build wealth to retire. Forget the focus on making money. This leads to wrong choices overall. This is the only way to send sufficient resources ahead for your destination arrival. The only way for you to fund each part of the Asset Reservoir specifically, is to budget by paying yourself first. I suggest you think of each goal having its own *Cookie Jar*. Be sure you are saving enough in each Cookie Jar to pay for the goal when it comes time. You fill your Asset Reservoir with these separate Cookie Jars. This viewpoint helps eliminate unintentionally using dollars from one goal for something else that pops up. This method gives you a capability to make choices when you see the impact the choices have on all your goals.

Also in the middle of the Road Map, you consider what to do if the trip does not go as planned—bring extra money, spare tire, the tent repair kit when camping—recall the Risk Management tools that we discussed for a financial journey. Risk management protects the net worth that makes up wealth. Risk management protects those Cookie Jars.

Once you have addressed everything from right to left, then you live on what is left. You do not need to keep detailed records about what you spend on a daily basis. Money is meant to be spent. However, now you can feel better about it because you have your first dollars going first towards what you have determined to be most important to you. Now you can live on the Left side of the Road Map knowing that your Standard of Individual Living is supportable today and you have addressed tomorrow's issues as well. Living today is less stressful once you know how to address all the issues that have bothered you.

CHAPTER 12

Already There—Retired?

Wealth is not measured by how fast you burn through dollars now; but how long those dollars last when you are not working.

You might say, "I am already retired." Do you think you have no more destinations, no other goals? Do you think your Odyssey is complete? That is too narrow a view. That might work for this year, but will it work next year, the next, and the next? Even if not yet retired, you should still read this chapter. Because you want to be retired someday and you need to understand the issues before you get there.

For the purpose of this book, I will define a pension plan as a plan where the employing company manages the assets to deliver a *defined benefit* to you. Hence, they are Defined Benefit (DB) programs or plans. They bring in the paid experts to determine what has to be distributed for each retiree's pension from the plan on a mandatory basis. They make the actuarial calculations needed to figure out how large an asset base is required to pay all the pensions. The company brings in the experts to manage the money. Most importantly, the company is required to add money from current company profits when there are shortfalls to pay the future pensions. This is assuming the company is solvent. Sometimes bankruptcy or lack of profits prevents the company from making the contributions that are required to keep the plan solvent. Yes, there is a government support plan. However, benefits to retirees have a maximum limit, which may mean a pay cut to retirees for troubled pension plans.

In reality, most of today's retirement programs are Defined Contribution (DC) plans. In many ways, you, not the company, manage the plan. The *contribution is defined*, not the benefit or payment, hence the name Defined Contribution. When you stop earning due to retirement or health, you cannot add any more to the retirement plan. The responsibility for funding the plan has been shifted to your shoulders! You are given the investment choices, but that is not the issue. You become the default expert with your self-managed retirement assets. You determine how the assets should be properly invested, when the assets are in trouble actuarially (in other words, when you have to *add* more from your current income to keep the benefit on track), and when to reduce distributions. You also confront the reality of not being able to add to the assets once you stop working, a big problem when you are already retired. People still believe they can do all of this by themselves?

Why Professional Advice?

There are two components to managing a Defined Contribution plan. First, is the management of the investments inside the portfolio, the analysis, selection, buying and selling of specific stocks, bonds, mutual funds, and so forth. All of these disciplines are full-time jobs, many requiring or benefiting from professional education and credentials. Second is management of the portfolio itself, the withdrawals, and timing of those withdrawals from the portfolio. Here probability analysis of market conditions and actuarial considerations come in handy. Professionals are paid to answer the questions: How long is the money going to last? How should the portfolio be constructed to last?

People get worried about how long their money will last, and then tend to take more risk than they are comfortable with to get the higher yield or return to force the portfolio into longer life. This trap snares many, and is one that professional advice can avoid. Companies get professionals, you should too! For all these reasons, your portfolio for retirement is too important for you *not* to consider using credentialed advisors. You cannot afford to make mistakes because you cannot mend the portfolio anymore once retired. Using a credentialed advisor minimizes the chance for error. However, it does not eliminate risk, market declines, or innocent errors.

Companies bring in the experts, so why don't you? Companies can add more money when the plan comes up short. You cannot once you are retired. You need to know the issues and understand the possibilities to solve them before finding yourself in that predicament. Not many people realize this, especially if they are still working. On the other hand, many retired people come to realize this too late, then they become too conservative and worry about protecting principal and living off of the interest only. Then, their assets fail to earn the returns required to avoid the shrinkage that they so fear in the first place.

Still a Future—Even When Retired

Whether you are retired or still working, you are still concerned about growing tomorrow's money. There are still years to consider in the future. You still have to get to other destinations. You want to be around years from now—right? Retirement might be divided into beginning, middle, and end stages. In other words, just because you are retired today does not mean you forget about 5, 10 or even more years from now. Your portfolio needs to be structured for later destinations. When you get there in the future, income will pay the expenses.

There should be a reserve pot. This reserve pot is not touched unless math shows that the portfolio is being stressed by withdrawals in adverse markets. Managing assets while retired should make you realize how important this task is. When you run out of shares, you have run out of money! Negative dollar cost averaging begins to work. Moreover, unlike in the accumulation years, you cannot add more money when you are retired.

Overall, your checkbook supports the standard of living expenses you have in retirement, with your portfolio transferring money to the checkbook each month. The checkbook is part of the income orientation of the portfolio. You still need growth as part of the asset preservation and inflation-fighting orientation.

You may think you are at your destination. In reality, in retirement you have arrived at just another day on the Left side of the Road Map. There are still years ahead of you, so really you are still traveling through the middle of the Road Map too. That means other components still apply. What is still at risk if something goes wrong? What if you are successful? Chapters 1–11 of The Wealth Odyssey still apply. Figure 12.1 shows a modified WORM for retirement. Essentially the layout is the same, with a *current situation and a future* set of destinations, with the required asset base to make it all happen. In this case, the Asset Reservoir supports the current situation, but must also support the future (yes, there is *still* a future!). The point: While farther along the Wealth Odyssey path, the major principles of sound financial planning and management still apply.

Figure 12.1: The Wealth Odyssey Road Map in Retirement

Starting Point:
Current Cashflow
Local Area
Familiar Budget

Route of Travel:
Financial Tools

Destination:
Cashflow for
Goals and Aspirations

Wealth = Net Worth
(Money at Work)

• Little/No Working Income
• Social Security/Pension
• Most Expenses funded from Assets and Asset Returns

Funding for Future
(There is still a future!)

Debt
Progress Line
Assets

Risk Management
Estate Plan

Budget
Income & Expenses

Assets support most expenses

Today's Standard of Living Expenses

Retirement Goals and Aspirations

Education (Grandchildren)
Travel
Big (Purchases)
Retired

Future Standard of Living Expenses

Developed by Better Financial Education 2002. Okay to reprint with this disclosure clearly visible.
Source book: Wealth Odyssey: The Essential Road Map to Reach Your Financial Goals
Modifications not authorized without permission from Better Financial Education.

Figure 12.1 The Wealth Odyssey Road Map in Retirement

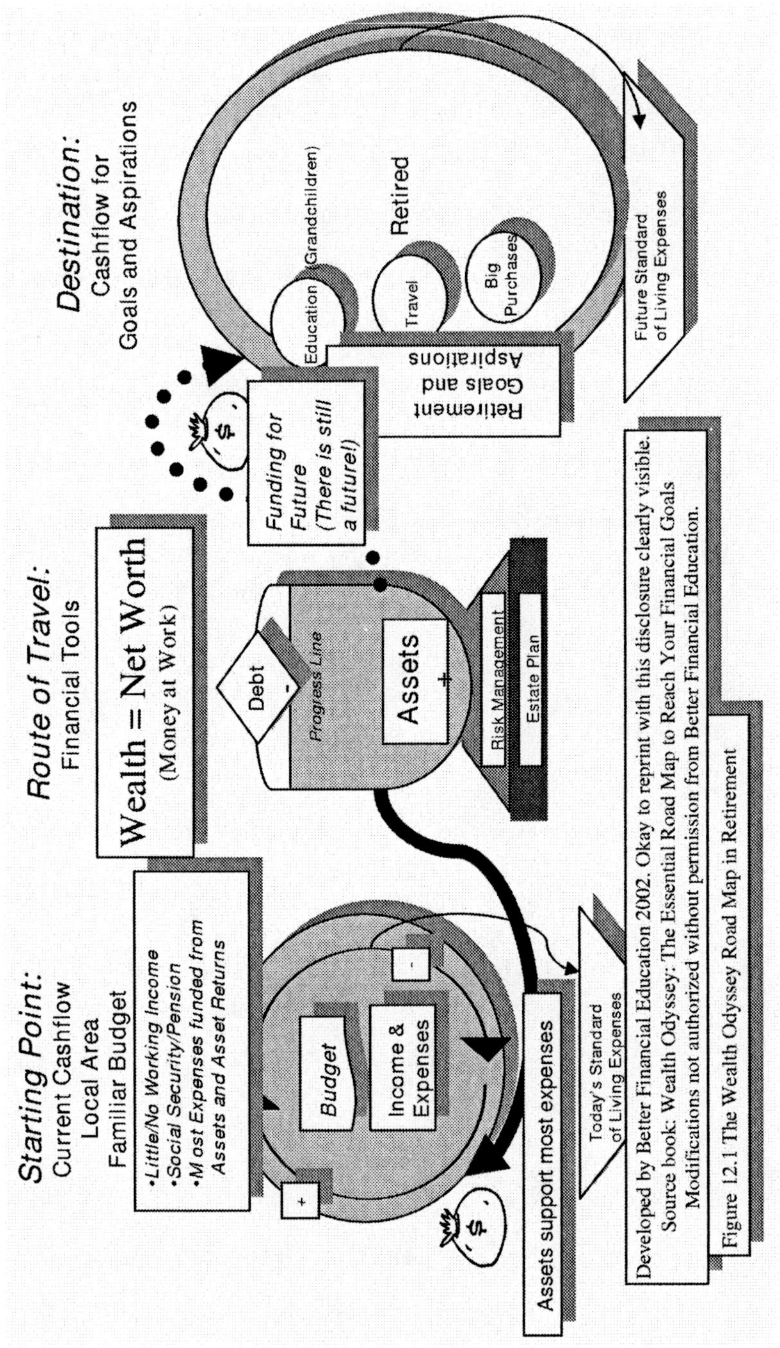

People often ask for specific suggestions in a book. I cannot offer any because I do not know you or your situation. It is no different from you calling a radio show to have quadruple bypass heart surgery. You probably would not do this. I suggest you take your money as seriously as you take your health. Be prudent. For the details, the books listed in Appendix E should be helpful.

Scenic Side Trip 12.1: What Can Money Do During Withdrawal?

You are retired now. Maybe you have inherited money. Alternatively, you are a widow or widower with a life insurance payment. Possibly, you have won the lottery. You have learned to handle sums of money between paychecks, become an expert at spending it all between those pay periods, or even faster! More *month* left at the end of the money! So what happens when people get a sum of money? Habit kicks in and, more often than not, they spent it too fast. How can you figure out if you are spending too much from your portfolio?

The Wealth Rule gives a decent starting place to determine appropriate withdrawals. Starting out, figure that they should be no more than 5 percent of the value annually. *Less is even better.* Therefore, for each $100,000 you should withdraw no more than $5,000 per year to pay your living expenses. Less is obviously better to improve the chances the money will last as long as you do! If you have $400,000, it would support no more than $20,000 of withdrawals for spending needs that year.

Retirement sums. Inheritances. Lottery. Life insurance payments. It does not matter where the money comes from for the rule works the same. Money does not know where it came from. No more than $5,000 per year for each $100,000 you have. You just need to have a realistic expectation of what that money is able to do. You can spend it all at once, or make it last forever.

The Wealth Rule works as a starting place to determine how much you would need for retirement in today's dollars. You can work it backwards. If your current income is $40,000 for example, then 40,000 divided by 5 percent equals $800,000. Another way to get the solution: 40,000 divided by 5,000 equals 8. Eight times each $100,000 from the rule above equals $800,000 total need. It does not matter how you work it. This Wealth Rule works to determine what amount of income you can get from an asset base. In other words, what amount of assets do you need to generate what amount of income?

You also can work the formula backwards to determine what happens if the money is not there for your family because you die. Example: the same $40,000 salary and the need for $800,000 in salary replacement when you retire. If you die you do not have the time to save for it. Therefore, the missing money comes by way of life insurance. Add to the income replacement cost any other desires you have, such as paid-off debt, paid-for education, etc., for the total amount of life insurance needed. It does not have to be any more confusing than that. Example: mortgage $250,000; college $75,000; credit card and car loans $25,000, plus the $800,000 income replacement and you get $1,150,000 insurance needed. Debts are paid and the balance remains to provide the missing income.

Clearly, if you had a sum of money, you could quit working; that is, if you had enough $100,000 increments to replace your annual salary. That is how it works for retirement. As I said earlier, money does not know where it came from; retirement savings, life insurance, the lottery, or inheritance. All it knows is that it is a sum of money. Money managed well as a portfolio can generate the same dollar distribution regardless of the source. Assets form wealth, and wealth supports a given standard of living.

These examples are starting points and are meant to demystify part of the planning concerns you have. They need to be modified based on the facts of your specific situation and desires you have. It is important to realize that the 5 percent figure above is a rate of withdrawal, not the rate of return, which can vary and disrupt the rule.

Several issues of *The Journal for Financial Planning,* an industry publication, have had articles addressing sustainable withdrawal rates based on various portfolio compositions. This area of research and study continues to be refined. See Appendix F.

Chapter 13
Your Wealth Odyssey Tour Guide

Without being guided; without being shown how to do it, "it" will not happen.

Whether you do it yourself as an individual investor or choose to use a credentialed advisor, it does not limit the utility of this book. My experience shows that the vast majority of people do not know where they are trying to go, or what to focus on. This is through no fault of theirs. Where would they have learned to think this way? Neither the mindset nor the appropriate sets of skills are taught anywhere, and the last time I checked, neither will financial knowledge descend out of the sky! This book provides a framework to help anyone determine, on his or her own, how to proceed. The book provides the Road Map to put it all together. You must be able to determine your main concerns and goals. Until you have thought about these first, no one can help you. You do not want someone else to determine your goals and concerns for you, because only you can know what they are. It is just like taking a trip. You, not the travel agent, determine where you want to go.

Bigger Reservoirs Require Better Management

Today you may be able to manage a small boat; in other words, a few assets. However, you want the boat to grow, to get bigger! That means that it is likely that it will become too big to manage on your own at some point in time. You want to remain the owner of the boat to control where it goes, but you should not have to be both captain and crew to get it there. In fact, the captain and crew work for the owner. As your assets grow, you should remain in charge, but do not try to run the whole ship by yourself. Get an experienced captain and be sure they understand that they work for you, and that they go where you want to go. The captain runs the ship and ensures the ship gets you to your destination. What's more, you can enjoy the life onboard en route and at your destination because the captain and crew are taking care of the details.

In the real world, there have been some problems with the use of professional financial services and financial planners. They fall into two camps. First, the phrase *financial planner* is not a specific but a generic label. To become clearer on the generic term financial planner and the many flavors thereof, please refer to Appendix D and the *teacher* analogy raised later in this chapter. These references will help you understand what the planner does and how they do it.

The second problem comes from failing to think about your life's goals ahead of time. You walk into a financial planner's office with absolutely no idea what you are trying to accomplish with your money. Your focus in the past has been on *where* to put the money, not why, not how to make the funds available in the first place. Your focus is on what this book calls the mode of transportation. This makes it too easy for salespeople. They too focus on the mode of transportation because that is their product! They give lip service to your goals, but the focus is still on where to put your money now. If you do not have goals, they are happy to suggest a few.

How do you avoid this? You can go it alone, that is, if you do not mind a steep learning curve, reinventing the wheel, and making costly errors. You are the chairperson—you make the decisions. You set the destinations. If you use a credentialed advisor, you need to understand the advisor's philosophy. Is it the same as yours? Even so, his or her destination and goals will be different from yours. You need to be sure you are being helped to your destination. You should ask, "Does your philosophy support my Road Map?" All of these elements are critical. It is okay if the advisor specializes in one area of the Road Map. You may recognize this and decide to become a general contractor, finding other credentialed advisors to fill in the gaps. You can coordinate the effort between them all. The credentialed advisor's value is guiding you to recognize what it is you are really trying to do to reach your goals; to show you how to achieve those goals; and to assist you as you work through each of the elements in your Road Map to arrive at your Destinations.

Planning Takes More Time than Selling

You do not want instant answers. Many people look for specific answers from general sources. They look in books, on television, through radio, newspapers, magazines, etc. General sources do not know you, or know where you are currently, or where it is you are trying to go. It takes time to plan a trip properly, does it not? It takes time for proper financial planning as well. You need time to determine where you are going; meanwhile the credentialed advisor needs time to learn about you and your destination and to determine the methods to get you there. *Planning takes time—selling does not.* If your advisor is in a rush, he is probably selling. This is true regardless of the advisor's credentials. Of course, procrastination can accomplish nothing either; *analysis paralysis* generates the illusion of accomplishment. On the other hand, thinking and learning do not actually get you started. Doing something with what you have learned is what gets you started. In addition, remember to keep things flexible so you can change what you have done in the past to keep up with life's changes in the future.

Are All Teachers the Same?

Let us say you ask someone what he or she does for a living, and are told, "I'm a teacher." Natural questions you then ask are what do you teach? Do you teach in high school or elementary? Where do you teach? In other words, you recognize that there are many different kinds of teachers. You ask someone this and he or she says, "I'm a financial planner." Now you stop. You assume you *know* what they do. Nevertheless, you really do not—because you did not ask further questions to determine any differences, as you did with the teacher. Generic financial planners typically are just that, generic. They use a sales process that a sales organization teaches them and they are paid and motivated through sales commissions.

Most credentialed advisors specialize in certain areas of financial planning and/or financial tools. They have experience requirements to get, and keep, their credential. They have initial and ongoing education requirements to get their credential. The credential at least tells you they have had specialized education and they have experience. Because they specialize, it is likely they do not do everything. It is the old saying, jack-of-all-trades, and master of none. You need to ask what it is they do, or do not, specialize in. Why? So that you can find someone, who does do that part for you if you need it. Does the credentialed advisor refer you to others? If so, he or she recognizes how the specialties of others fit together with his or her own to assist you better. What is the fee arrangement if any, i.e., is the advisor compensated in return for a referral? These answers tell you as much about credentialed advisors as what they tell you about what they can do for you.

The Difference Between Travel Agent and Tour Guide

The sales process typically focuses on the entity, in other words, the sales organization or company with which the advisor is associated. The planning process focuses on you. The travel agent books the trip and sends you on your way, but does not go along. The tour guide goes on the journey with you, knows the route, knows the terrain and modes of transportation to cross it. The tour guide makes the trip more enjoyable and points things out along the way that you would not have noticed otherwise. The tour guide can concentrate on the details so you can enjoy the journey, and so you can enjoy arriving at the destination.

For all the above reasons, I suggest you find a credentialed advisor if you are inclined to search for assistance. What kind of advisor should you look for? Review Appendix D to compare the different kinds of advisors available. As of the writing of this book, the investor education area of the NASD's website (www.nasd.com) has a section called *Understanding Professional Designations*. This is important to do before walking in the door. An advisor's business card or letterhead should have his or her professional designation(s) on it. You are in charge of the destination and well as the process. The credentialed advisor must understand that he works for you.

Fee Versus Free

A brief comment comparing fee-based and commission-based planners may also help. This is a great debate among those in the financial industry. Most of the debate focus on what is better for the advisor rather than what is good for you. You probably need to start with a commission-based advisor. When most people start, they do not have much in the way of assets. The advisor must earn a living somehow, so paying commissions probably makes sense. This may seem unpleasant, but you need to start somewhere. Otherwise, you never will accumulate anything.

You could pay fees initially, but does it make sense to pay an advisor, for example $2,000 a year, if you are just starting with $100 a month to invest? Probably not. Once you have accumulated assets it may make sense to switch to fee-based planners or look at some combination of compensation forms. At that point, fees are small relative to assets.

Some credentialed advisors accept both fees and commissions. They are probably working both with clients still accumulating wealth and those who have already had some success. Which is better? It depends on you and your situation, and your comfort with the advisor and his or her ability to execute on your goals.

The bottom line: Should you decide you want help, be sure it is the kind of help you need. You need to have some idea where you are trying to get to so that the credentialed advisor knows how to assist you in getting there, and can guide you once you arrive too.

How to Begin *Your* Wealth Odyssey

You may have a sense of unresolved questions: "So where do I go from here? How do I start?" I have mapped out a process to help you with these questions. I provide you with Appendix C as a *real life* review with people whose names are changed. It serves to transition your traditional financial thinking with the aid of the Wealth Odyssey Road Map, SOIL, Wealth Rule and Progress Line. Appendices A and B are provided as a review and quick reference, both for the case study and later as you apply the principles in this work to your life. The *Five Steps Taken* section of Appendix C summarizes crucial stages you need to take, especially if you are doing this yourself. These are critical steps before you talk to a tour guide as well.

So what is the correct strategy? Pursue a prudent combination of uncertainty; this is what asset allocation and diversification means. The future remains uncertain for everyone. Hence, monitoring and refinements are important. You refine things once the future uncertainty becomes clear in the present and the past. Hindsight can be perfect, but nobody can know anything ahead of time with any degree of certainty. There are no shortcuts.

An odyssey is a journey, or it could be wandering. Which do you prefer? Do not wander. You must journey with one or more destinations in mind. Have your journey well thought out. You also need to understand where you are right now. You measured that with your SOIL. Then you can set your course and begin your journey. Do not confuse a mode of transportation with a destination. You cross the Road Map from where you are to get to your destination by the use of modes of transportation. You budget the resources to accumulate the assets to finish your journey. Measure your progress along the way with the Progress Line and Wealth Rule. Stop the wandering; make it a journey with a purpose. You also need to consider the hazards along the way. In other words, you consider all the elements on the Road Map working from the Right- to the Left-Side. Use the Road Map. It will help you find your way. Decide where you are trying to go. Determine where you are today. Connect the two on the Road Map. Then you can answer the question: Where are you are trying to go with *your* money?

Just because you may feel you have arrived does not mean the trip is over. Often it means the trip is just beginning. Moreover, just because you finished reading this book does not mean your job is finished. Financial planning is a continuous process. Read about Carol and Carl Doe in Appendix C to see how to apply this process, and these concepts, to make your journey easier.

Today is the first day of the rest of your life. You still have much of your journey ahead of you. What are your destinations? How are you going to arrive at those destinations? How are you going to monitor your progress between where you are today and where you want to be? It is now time to embark on *your* wealth odyssey. Bon voyage.

APPENDIX A.

The Wealth Odyssey Road Map (WORM)

Figure A.1: The Wealth Odyssey Road Map

Starting Point: Current Cashflow Local Area

Route of Travel: Financial Tools

Destination: Cashflow for Goals and Aspirations

Work = Income

Funding

Budget

Income & Expenses

+

Today's Standard of Living Expenses

Wealth = Net Worth
(Money at Work)

Debt
–

Assets
+

Progress Line

Risk Management

Estate Plan

Funding

$

Intermediate Goals and Aspirations

Education

Vacations

Big Purchases

Retirement

Future Standard of Living Expenses

Developed by Better Financial Education 2002. Okay to reprint with this disclosure clearly visible. Source book: Wealth Odyssey: The Essential Road Map to Reach Your Financial Goals Modifications not authorized without permission from Better Financial Education.

Figure A.1 The Wealth Odyssey Road Map (WORM)

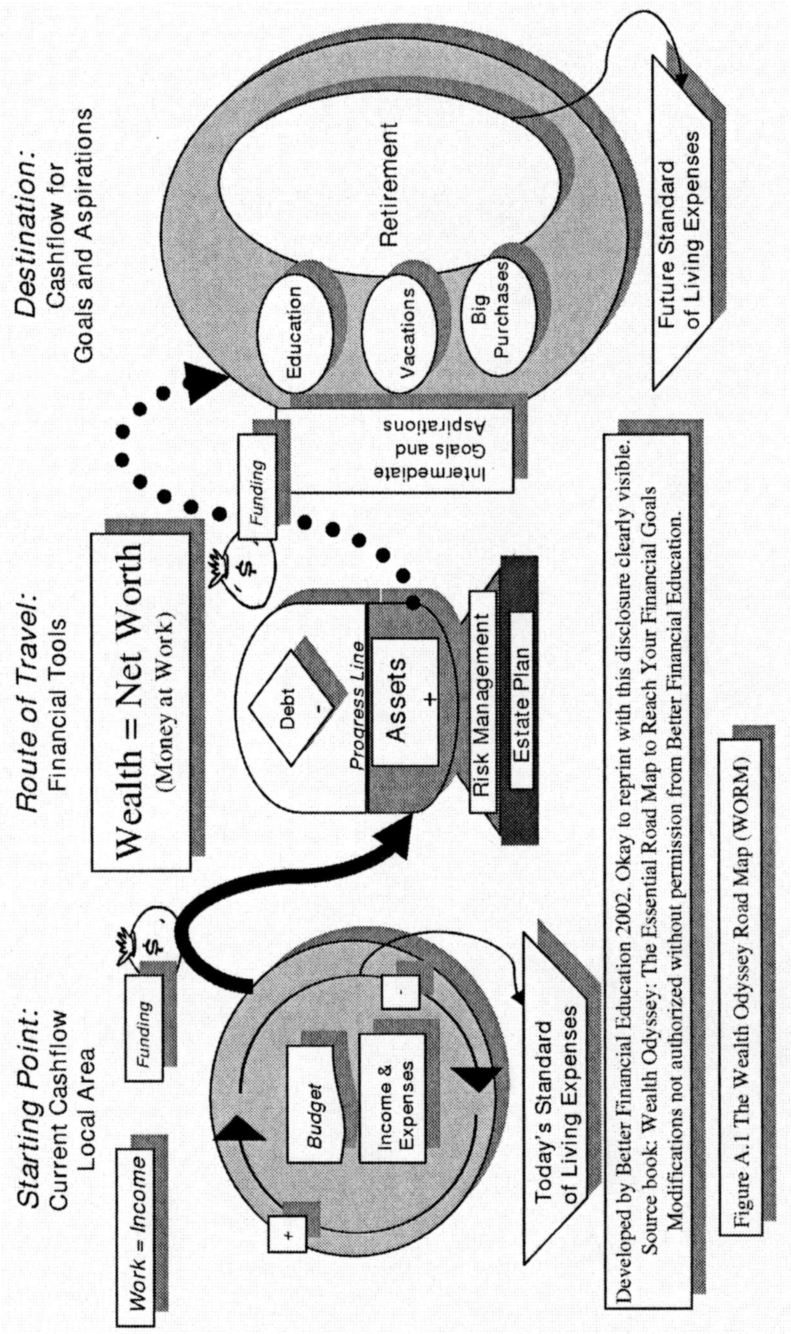

APPENDIX B

Wealth Rule Examples

To develop your understanding of the Wealth Rule, here are a few more examples.

Retirement Example

Using a 5 percent withdrawal rate, which assumes replacement based on long-term return on underlying assets of approximately 5 percent, each $100,000 of assets in the Asset Reservoir can be converted to $5,000 per year in cash. This $5,000 represents proceeds from income and growth in the underlying assets (recall the *total return* concept from Chapter 10). Working backwards, if you need $30,000 per year to support your retirement SOIL, you will nominally need $600,000 in your Asset Reservoir ($600,000 x 5 percent = $30,000).

However, you are not done at this point. Your Social Security (and/or pension benefit—the Defined Benefit kind) reduces the amount you need to self-fund. Suppose your projected benefit is $1,000 a month, or $12,000 per year. That reduces your *net* retirement need to $18,000 ($30,000 – $12,000). Working backwards again through the Wealth Rule, that implies a required asset base of $360,000 ($18,000 *divided* by 5 percent).

That may not sound so bad, but now recall that to the extent that your retirement accounts make up much of your Asset Reservoir, withdrawals from those accounts are taxable. Therefore, to produce the $18,000 per year of after-tax income necessary to support your retirement SOIL, you may need to withdraw $22,000 per year. Once again, working backwards, you now need a retirement Asset Reservoir of $440,000 ($22,000 divided by 5 percent). It is always prudent to err on the conservative side, meaning erring towards the higher required amount.

Life Insurance Example

Life insurance works the same way. Instead of accumulating the assets in the Asset Reservoir to support retirement over time, in this situation the *time needed to accumulate those assets is lost* due to an unforeseen event. The element lost is the income source to pay the current SOIL *and* to accumulate the Asset Reservoir for retirement, a *double whammy* for the survivors. So if today $60,000 per year is required to support your part of the SOIL (your contribution only, do not include your spouse's here), working backwards through the Wealth Rule implies a required Asset Reservoir of $1,200,000 to replace this lost source of income. Do you actually have these assets? No. Instead, use insurance to fill the Asset Reservoir with that amount in the event of death so those who still need the support will have it. Remember, insurance is the asset you do not have for the obligation you do have.

Do we need to make the same adjustments as made above for retirement for things like Social Security and taxes? Social Security may apply if there are minor children and they meet qualification requirements. In addition, a survivor spouse benefit starts at the age of 60. On the other hand, there may be some other income from investments or from a surviving spouse's income. Remember, though, that the example is talking about the deceased spouse's lost contribution, so this already has adjusted for the surviving spouse's income. Are there taxes due on life insurance benefits? Life insurance proceeds are generally not subject to income tax (although, once invested, earnings are). The calculation is quite similar to that for retirement because it is a large amount for a long period. Remember to add to this *lost income* figure the amount needed for other sums to pay off debt, future education of children, and other goals.

General Wealth Rule Comments

Here are some general comments on the use of the Wealth Rule. First, the distribution percentage is very important. A lower withdrawal rate will require more assets to support it, but will be more likely to be sustainable over the long haul. For example, 4 percent would be ideal to allow the wealth a better opportunity to continue to grow and be able to last years longer than the 5 percent withdrawal rate. This is intuitive, the less you take for withdrawals, the longer the money will last. Second, this is a distribution or withdrawal rate only; it is not in any way related to the rate of return on the wealth asset.

The Wealth Rule calculates what you need, at minimum, to support your SOIL. It does not include reserves. During retirement, having a sum of wealth in reserves, for example 18 to 36 months (the correct amount is based on your comfort level), would be wise to weather the cyclical nature of any asset value and the unpredictability of expenses. While the underlying assets rise in value, you should keep your withdrawals unchanged if possible. While the underlying asset declines, withdrawals can come from the reserve pool.

Managing asset withdrawals, or *distribution,* can be a tricky process. Professional help from a credentialed advisor knowledgeable in the topic of withdrawals may be in order.

APPENDIX C

Case Study: A Typical Family with Multiple Goals

This case study will look at a typical family (names changed) and their finances. It will illustrate the difficult and often conflicting choices one has in personal finance. The case study wrap-up—Five Steps Taken—summarizes the steps to address financial planning using the WORM and the concepts introduced in this work.

Your numbers are likely to be different, but your daily problems are not. The point is not how big or small the numbers here are relative to yours, but to demonstrate how to relate the concepts through real life examples. Each family evaluates their own concerns, prioritizes them, and prioritizes available resources, determining a combination to form their own unique answer and their own unique destination.

No one answer is right or wrong. Why not right or wrong? The answer depends on the person. That has been a major theme of this book. Each person makes choices based on his or her priorities in life. People err in viewing each issue in isolation from the other issues. Realize that taking one issue at a time you are unlikely to achieve any of the others. However, in combination, you are likely to get farther. The case is greater than the parts.

The past does not predict the future. Indeed, the future is often much different from what the past would suggest. I am not using any specific rate of return in this example because I evaluate the issues probabilistically. Answers are not likely to be singular but can occur over a range of possible outcomes.

Although our case study is a couple, the overall issues do not change for singles. The priority of the issues may change. Children's education, for example, may not be relevant. Simply skip over those parts of the case study. In reality, single or married, this is how it works in life. You simply skip those potential issues that do not concern you, or are lower in priority to other concerns. In addition, as the wheel of life turns, things change. What was once no concern can rapidly become a higher priority. Remember, people decide their own destination. Finally, this case study does not cover all concerns that are possible in life to enable this case study to fit in this book! Common concerns are addressed, not *all* concerns.

A 40-something married couple forms the base for the example. They own their home. They are both employed, though he just changed employers. They have two children. Their list of concerns seems to be the typical, impossible list all people have, along with the dilemma of how to apply their limited paychecks to achieve everything they want to achieve. You will see these issues brought together. Moreover, things will evolve over time; nothing from your past is the same today as it was then. Nothing in your future will be the same as you plan it today. You monitor your goals and change them as you travel through life.

The below financial topics and concerns are covered in no particular order. The format used throughout will be a recap of the current situation and the shortages evident in each situation. It will remain up to the individuals themselves in this case to prioritize their concerns once they have reviewed their situation. This is true for *anyone, including you*. Only you can determine what your priorities are and which goals you want to reach; in other words, what your own destinations should be.

Case Facts

Carol and Carl Doe are in their early 40s and have two children, Jane and John. Carl works in retail and Carol is a salesperson. Together they have a monthly gross income of $6,500. Everyone is in good health today.

Below is a recap of the allocation of some of their money today. Note that the list details how the money is *currently* used. It does not say how the couple has decided to use the money later after they have developed their list of concerns and subsequently prioritized that list. I have not provided their list and solutions because the possible combination of priorities and goals is limitless.

- $100 currently per month to a mutual fund
- $200 currently per month extra to the mortgage
- $400 per month paid to service credit cards (available in two years when credit cards are paid off)
- $871 per month for car loans (available in two to three years when both car loans are paid off)
- $58 per month for life insurance

Reserves

Current situation: They have $1,500 in a money market fund and $1,000 in savings for a total of $2,500. They also have $7,500 in a mutual fund, to which they have been adding $100 a month. This money is set aside for the education expenses for Jane and John. However, should an emergency arise, they will need this money to cover it. Therefore, they have a total of $10,000 for emergency use if needed. They realize that this would adversely affect the education opportunities for both if this happened.

Shortage analysis: They determined that their minimum expenses that must be covered each month amount to $4,900. They eliminated money going to entertainment, retirement plans, education, home maintenance, clothing, etc. to arrive at this figure. Her job is stable; however, his company is subject to periodic mergers and acquisitions, and his job might not continue in some case. He estimates it would take about eight months to find another job. Multiplying eight months times $4,900 per month equals $39,200 needed for total reserves; $39,200 minus the current $10,000 equals a shortage of $29,200 (if the $7,500 in funds set aside for education are not touched the shortage would rise to $36,700). They write these amounts down on paper as a *concern*.

Education for Children: Ages 14 and 8

Current situation: They have $7,500 in a mutual fund and add $100 a month. The children both want to attend a state university for which current tuition, room, and board is $6,000 a year.

Shortage analysis: The tuition in four years (for the oldest) could range between $8,000 and $10,000 each year. In 10 years (for the youngest), these figures could be between $12,000 and $16,000. These tuition costs are likely to increase each of the four years they attend the university. The total tuition for the oldest is about $35,900 and for the youngest is approximately $56,300. If the oldest uses the mutual fund money, she is still short approximately $26,000 today, requiring around $350 a month to save up the difference. The youngest is short the entire amount today since the money would be used up by the oldest. This shortfall needs about $300 a month to save up for his balance. Carol and Carl realize that if they wait, they will have to come up with between $8,000 ($667 a month) to $16,000 ($1,334 a month) each year their children are in college. They write all these amounts down on their paper as a concern.

Debt

Current situation: They have been paying an extra $200 per month on their mortgage that will pay off the mortgage six years ahead of schedule. They plan on living in the home until the youngest completes college. They have two car loans with balances totaling $20,000 with total payments of $871. Finally, they have $8,700 in credit card debt for which they have been making a monthly payment of $400.

Shortage analysis: They have wondered if making an extra mortgage payment is a good idea. They write this down as a concern to decide this later, after they have a complete list from which they can make a good decision. Their cars are two and three years old with three years and two years left on each loan, respectively. They decide that they should keep these cars as long as they can, hopefully another 8 to 10 years each, and write this down as a goal. They also write down as a goal to continue to pay down their credit cards at the current rate and not add any further expenses. They will start to use their checking account debit card for purchases instead of credit cards. They write down that they will use the $400 a month to address their concerns in approximately two years time when they estimate they will have paid off the cards; and the $871 as available when the car loans have been paid.

Retirement

Current situation: There is $8,700 in Carl's company retirement plan. He contributes 6 percent (usually around $200 a month) because this is the company's maximum for matching amounts. Carol's company has no retirement plan. They want to maintain their current standard of living (SOIL) of $75,600 a year.

Shortage analysis: They estimate that their true standard of living expenses without work related expenses is $70,000 per year today. They use the Wealth Rule to calculate the assets needed to generate that amount of income (Each $100,000 of assets may generate $5,000 per year in income). Their $70,000 SOIL divided by $5,000 equals 14. Fourteen multiplied by $100,000 means they should accumulate $1,400,000 in assets for retirement. With their current contribution rate and the employer match, they had estimated that they would accumulate about $1,000,000. That seemed to be a big number, especially considering that $70,000 is just 7 percent of it. Now they realize that 7 percent probably will be too much to try to take from their assets during their retirement, especially considering that they will not be able to make up any shortfalls when markets decline. They also realize that $70,000 is today's standard of living. Certainly, before they reach 65, the cost of living will go up. They need to have extra in their retirement account for increasing cost-of-living expenses as they age. They realize that when they get promotions, bonuses, and pay raises that the money should be put into retirement accounts, both personal and company-provided. This will do two things: 1) put aside more dollars that they will need for retirement, and 2) keep their standard of living (SOIL) reasonable. If they were to spend that extra money, they would get used to a higher lifestyle, which would be harder to support and require even more assets for retirement. They annotate their list with these thoughts. Once they see that they have the assets projected to maintain today's standard of living, then they can work on coordinating improvements in today's lifestyle along with saving to maintain their standard of living in the future. The numbers tell them that they are doing about two-thirds of what they need to do to sustain today's lifestyle.

Premature Death—Either Spouse

Current situation: Carl has $50,000 employer group coverage and another $50,000 life insurance policy through a public insurance company. Carol also has $50,000 through the same public insurance company. Their premiums are $58 per month.

Shortage analysis: They estimate the mortgage and debt to be $100,000, the amount Carl has for group life insurance coverage. He figures his income is higher so he could live on less if something happens to Carol. They realize that should something happen, college education for the children would suffer because neither of them could save enough without the other's help and income. Therefore, they list the total from their education analysis, as an additional amount they would need, still not covered by life insurance. Carol and Carl each need an additional $92,200 ($35,900 plus $56,300) in life insurance to pay for education if something happens before either child finishes college. Then they realize that this only covers debt and the education goal. Their life insurance does not cover funeral expenses (estimated to be $8,000). It also does not replace the lost income. It does not help to be able to pay the mortgage and keep the house if the family cannot afford to pay the utilities and other normal living expenses. They realize that this is a big oversight. They use the Wealth Rule to calculate the assets for the sum of money to generate a certain income. Their incomes are Carol: $35,000 divided by $5,000 = 7 times $100,000 for a total life insurance income replacement need of $700,000; Carl: $40,000 divided by $5,000 = 8 times $100,000 for a total life insurance need for income replacement of $800,000.

They put on their concern list the amounts of the education asset shortfall and the income-replacement asset shortfall. They also know that Social Security would pay a survivor benefit to the children and the surviving spouse. However, they do not want to rely entirely on Social Security and decide to have it calculated in their plan as a *buffer* income for the family. They know Social Security won't provide for everything they need and it also stops when the children reach age 18.They also realize that the survivor won't have the ability to save as easily for their own retirement because they will be on just one reduced income. Again, Social Security can serve as a buffer. They mark on their priority list as an annotation the estimated family income from Social Security's annual statements received each year in the mail.

Employer Disability Insurance

Current situation: Carl has not elected to take the employer group long-term disability plan. Carol has no employer benefit for disability.

Shortage analysis: He realizes that injury or illness could be for a long term. He would use up his vacation days quickly and the short-term disability plan lasts only for a few months. He had no interest in the long-term plan because it only provided 50 percent of current wages anyway, and the benefit is taxable, so he would end up with even less after taxes. He could purchase an additional benefit to make the total benefit 65 percent of income. The benefits are not taxed because he pays the premiums with after-tax dollars. He had talked with a co-worker who worked with a disability specialist outside the company. The specialist designed a personal long-term disability program to make up the income shortfall between what the company's plan would provide and what they needed. His co-worker had also worked out a plan that would provide additional dollars to put into a retirement plan. Carol realizes that she has no coverage for this risk to her income. Carl and Carol put this issue on their list of concerns and realize they need to get more information about this risk that they never considered before. They are happy to hear that they can customize the plan outside the employer. Once they have a couple of customized quotes in front of them, they can further evaluate how this issue fits among their priorities and resources.

Living Trust, Or Wills

Current situation: They have no wills.

Shortage analysis: They realize that they are going through great effort to build wealth and to raise their children. They never stopped to think about the issues that would arise if something happened to them prematurely. Who would take care of the children? They always thought that her sister would. What would state law allow? Who would take care of the assets on behalf of the children? His brother was good with numbers and money. Again, what would state law allow? They have a home and children. They have money here and there. They put on their list that they need to talk with an attorney about all of this. They know what they would like to see happen, but the state would not recognize their wishes as legal since it is not in a recognized form.

Carol and Carl now have a completed list of concerns with amounts needed written next to each concern. Now they begin their discussion about the priorities they have for these concerns. They recognize they have limited resources and a long list of issues. By prioritizing these concerns they have realized what decisions they are comfortable with, and which of these concerns will get smaller, or no, funding until they have more income to allocate to them later. They have set up their bank account to send money automatically to everything on their list, with the amount they have decided on. They keep this developed list. It serves to remind them of the decisions they have made. It will also help to review it when they get pay raises, bonuses, or promotions, to be sure that they continue to address their goals, especially the ones that concern them the most. When they change the list later, they can revise it to keep it current with new changes.

Progress Line

Carl and Carol have diagrammed their situation and their concerns on a piece of paper in the form of a Road Map. See Figure C.1.

Figure C.1: The Doe Family Case Study

Destinations (Goals and Aspirations):
Retirement: $1,400,000
Reserves: $39,200
Tuitions: $35,900 + $56,300 or
                 $300 + $350/mo.
Vacations: Current budget (not on credit)

Retirement SOIL
$5,834

Retirement

Education   Vacations

Intermediate
Goals

Debt:
Home Mortgage $77,000
Cars $20,000
Credit Cards $8,700
Total: $105,700

Funding

Debt
−

Progress Line

Assets
+

Risk Management

Estate Plan

Funding:
Debt: $871/mo car loans
      $400/mo credit cards
Above debt $ available when paid off
      $200/mo extra on mortgage
Assets: $100/mo mutual fund
        $200/mo retirement plan
Risk Management: $58/mo Life Ins

Income $6,300

Budget

Income &
Expenses

+

Assets:
Home $200,000
Retirement plan $8,700
Mutual Fund $7,500
Reserves $2,500
Total: $218,700

SOIL $6,300
Minimum
Budget $4,900

Progress Line ("Net Worth"): With Home +$113,000; Without Home − $10,000

Figure Appendix C – The Doe Family Case Study

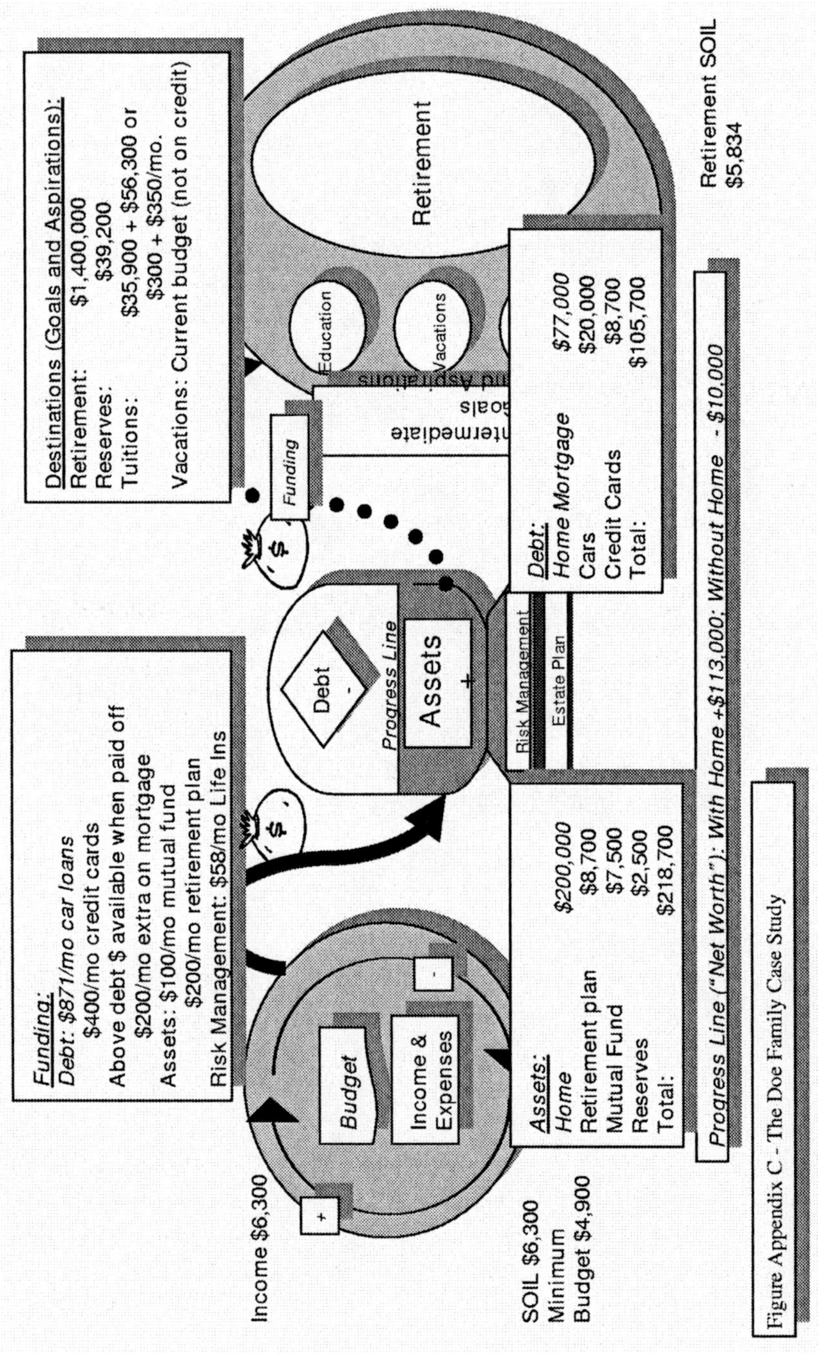

In addition to the annotations on their WORM (Figure C.1), Carol and Carl have made commitments to address numerous risk management topics: home and auto insurance, life insurance for both, disability insurance for both; and to talk with an attorney about wills, living trusts, and other legal documents needed.

Their Progress Line (net worth) is $113,000 ($218,700 minus $105,700) when they include their home. Excluding their home, their Progress Line is a *negative* $10,000. This alarms Carl and Carol, because it would mean they would have to sell the home under the current situation if something happens to their income. Non-home related debt far outpaces their non-home related assets. It is clear they need to prioritize their concerns to develop the list of their goals that they can address now with the resources they have available. They also recognize the need to pay attention to the other factors in the center of the WORM that support their assets, such as risk management and estate planning.

Fast Forward

Carol and Carl are now in their early 60s; the children are living on their own. Their gross income has grown to $105,000. They have $1,200,000 total in all their retirement plans. They are debt free. Their home is worth $450,000 now. They are considering moving to a smaller home and this move would net them $150,000 in cash and a paid-for new home from the sale. They both plan to work for about four more years and are currently putting $25,000 a year towards retirement. Therefore, their total assets would be $1,450,000 (4 times $25,000 plus $150,000 plus $1,200,000). Their standard of living is $105,000 minus the $25,000 they put towards retirement (they are not spending this on living expenses), or $80,000. The Wealth Rule suggests that they need $1,600,000. They are short $150,000 ($1,600,000 minus $1,450,000). Now they have a choice. They could work a few years longer than planned, allowing them to save up the difference through retirement plan contributions. Alternatively, they could look at how they could reduce living expenses by $7,500 a year ($150,000 times 5 percent which comes from the Wealth Rule). They need to list all their goals and things they would like to do once they retire to decide how to handle all of this.

Carl and Carol have not yet purchased Long Term Care Insurance. They had looked at it when they were younger but did not feel they had the money in their budget. They still do not. They realize that it is likely that one of them will need this kind of care, if not both. They call their credentialed advisor, determined not to procrastinate on this issue any longer. If one of them needs care, it will use up all of their resources and leave the other without sufficient assets for support. Neither wants to take this risk and they decide that self-insurance is no longer how they want to handle it. They will transfer the risk to a good insurance company. It occurs to them that they will begin to receive Social Security in a few years. They will use this to pay the premiums for this coverage. In the meantime, they will pay the premiums from current salaries and look to reduce expenses somewhere. They wish they had done this when they were younger when the premiums were lower. Now this concern has become a high priority for them.

Case Study Wrap-up—Five Steps Taken

This case illustrates the realities for Carl and Carol and others in similar circumstances—limited resources with many, and competing, goals. Here I continue to illustrate the overall financial planning *process* deployed in the Wealth Odyssey— really, the underlying message and *destination* for readers of this book.

Note the sequence of steps here. In *Step 1*—Carol and Carl confronted themselves with the necessity to develop a financial plan. They were uncomfortable with their current situation and their perception of their future, so they sat down and started mapping out their destinations, goals, college education, retirement, and so forth. As a financial planner, I have found this is one of the most difficult steps for people to take—*getting started*.

Once started, the Does worked through *Step 2*—the determination of current and future SOIL, and whether their SOIL made sense given current facts. By definition, their SOIL is unique to their situation, and must be fully understood, and corrected if necessary, before proceeding.

Step 3 employs the Wealth Rule to determine, based on SOIL, their financial targets required to reach their destinations. Once that number is in place, the planning continues to *Step 4*—building the Asset Reservoir and measuring progress through the Progress Line. Note that specific investment tools and vehicles are but a sidebar in the overall discussion; these *modes of transportation* are mere tactics supporting a much larger strategy.

Finally, in *Step 5*, the plan incorporates the *what-if* of risk management and estate planning, providing a path to reach the destination in the event that unforeseen events impede progress. Once this five-step process is complete, the Does can go on through life with a plan. While at times difficult, there is comfort in knowing where they are going, and in fact, they do end up reaching their destination, a feat that looked unlikely in the beginning. Note that their journey was unique to their situation; that no *canned answer* was available.

The Search for Correct Answers

TV, radio, newspapers, and magazines all imply there is an optimal answer to everything. There would be if we were all the same. That is not reality. And it ignores the fact that in life different goals compete for our limited resources. There is no one answer because it depends on what all the goals are. We all have different goals, so how could the answer be the same if the goal mix is different? Many people let others superimpose their opinion as to what their goals and priorities should be. A credentialed advisor should be looking at your situation primarily to help you determine your goals and the relative priority each has for you. This simple case study illustrates that complexity to some degree.

Some will attempt to find fault with this case study since there was no *answer* provided. Indeed, they will have missed the point, for until one determines what the priority of each goal is and resources the family is willing to apply to each goal, there is no answer. Many will try to superimpose their opinion as to what the answer is. Again, they miss the point. There is no correct answer until one determines what the priorities are in relation to the goals. Once this is determined, a solution begins to emerge. You cannot measure your progress against someone else's goals. You cannot get your answer from generic sources. You cannot get your answer from a sales organization. You get possible solutions, what I call *modes of transportation*, from those sources. Only after you have determined what you are trying to do will possible solutions become apparent. You cannot measure your progress against a generic index. What does it have to do with you? You measure your progress against your own goals using the Progress Line. The assets you have compared to the assets you need to support your goals, as calculated by the Wealth Rule, measure your progress.

APPENDIX D

Credentialed Advisor Designations

Consumers are confused enough about the various kinds of financial advisors and their credentials, so this Appendix is offered to clarify a few points.

Let us use Webster's dictionary for some important definitions here. A **degree** is an academic title awarded to one who has completed a given course of study. A **credential** is a basis for confidence. A **designation** is a given, or appointed, name or title. A **license** is the legal permission to operate, the authority given by federal or state governments to transact business, i.e. to sell securities or insurance. A **label** is something used to describe or identify something.

The terms financial advisor, financial planner, financial counselor, financial expert, etc. are *labels*. They are not designations, credentials, or anything else. Someone who passes a basic licensing exam in either, or both, securities or insurance can use such a label. Some who are unlicensed use these labels, too. There is no governing body for the use of a label. A *designation* is earned by 1) experience, 2) specific course study, and 3) a comprehensive exam or exams, and it may come from a title given by an employer, such as a bank or credit union. A designation forms the basis for a *credential*. A designation is maintained through continuing education granted through the credential's governing board and adherence to an ethical code. The credential is a designation granted by a governing body. The requirements for granting the credential, through design, give the client confidence in working with this professional.

This book uses the term *credentialed advisor* to distinguish between those with only a license and those who have gone beyond the initial license. Credentialed advisors go beyond legal minimums. In other words, the term makes a distinction between someone merely using a label under a license, and someone who has had a designation given by a governing body for the purposes of having additional qualifications to work with you. It provides the basis for confidence in their expertise. I emphasize the use of a credentialed advisor, not just a financial planner, for these reasons. You can verify a credentialed advisor's authenticity through regulatory agencies and the credential's governing organization websites or toll-free numbers. Your credentialed advisor can provide you with the information needed to verify his or her official status through these legitimate sources. Do not take their word for it, but verify their authenticity. I provide a list of some of these types of advisors below.

Financial planning is not purchasing something. Purchasing something is what you do to implement some part of your plan. Investment advice, tax advice, insurance advice, etc., are subsets that are tools in the overall process called financial planning. Discussing any one or two parts of the Road Map is not financial planning. For example, retirement planning looks at accumulating the resources to retire. Similarly, looking into insurance is just looking at that supporting part of the Road Map.

Financial planning is a process. Develop the plan through a process designed to assist you in determining where you are and where you are trying to get. The purpose of financial planning is to coordinate all the aspects of personal finance. In other words, to coordinate all the parts of the Road Map simultaneously. This is hard to do without a framework or viewpoint to visualize how all these personal finance elements come together and what their general purpose is.

The term, credentialed advisor, refers to those who have met experience requirements, a course of study, and have ongoing education requirements to maintain the credential. The designation applies to the name of the credential. There may be other designations that are granted through a course of study, but do *not* have any further requirement to maintain the designation once it has been received. An example would be Certified Fund Specialist (CFS).

This is a dynamic field with likely changes in the future. The list of credentials presented below is not all-inclusive, but has the most common designations the individual consumer may encounter. Ask the advisor for the website and contact information for the organization sponsoring any designation. Verify for yourself what the designation is and how it applies to your specific situation and needs. You can research many of these credentials further on the Internet through various search engines. One composite resource for professional designations is the National Association of Securities Dealers (NASD) website (www.nasd.com), offering an area called Understanding Professional Designations in its Investor Education section.

The following credentials require continuing study to maintain the designation through a specific and formal continuing education program:

- Certified Financial Planner (CFP)
- Certified Divorce Planner (CDP)

- Chartered Investment Management Consultant (CIMC)
- Chartered Financial Consultant (ChFC) and Charter Life Underwriter (CLU)
- Personal Financial Specialist (PFS)

These following designations are *accounting or tax related.* They also have continuing education requirements:

- Certified Public Accountant (CPA)
- Enrolled Agent (EA)

The next set of designations, once granted, generally have *no further requirement* to maintain knowledge or experience in the field of study through a specific continuing education program requirement:

- Certified Fund Specialist (CFS)
- Board Certified in Insurance (BCI)
- Board Certified in Securities (BCS)
- Board Certified in Estate Planning (BCE)
- Life Underwriter Training Council Fellow (LUTCF)
- Certified Senior Advisor (CSA)

APPENDIX E
Additional Reading and Research Sources

The following books and references are provided to help you broaden and develop your philosophical foundation and personal finance expertise.

Against the Gods. The Remarkable Story of Risk. Peter L. Bernstein. John Wiley & Sons, Inc., New York NY. 1998.

Affluenza. The All-Consuming Epidemic. John De Graaf, David Wann, Thomas H. Naylor. Berrett-Koehler Publishers Inc, San Francisco CA. 2002.

A Mathematician Plays the Stock Market. John Allen Paulos. Basic Books. New York NY. 2003.

Asset Allocation. Balancing Financial Risk. Roger C. Gibson. McGraw-Hill, New York NY. 2000.

The Birth of Plenty. How the Prosperity of the Modern World was Created. William Bernstein. McGraw-Hill, New York NY. 2004.

Complexity, Risk, and Financial Markets. Edgar E. Peters. John Wiley & Sons, Inc., New York NY. 1999.

Economics Explained. Everything You Need to Know about How the Economy Works and Where It's Going. Robert Heilbroner and Lester Thurow. Touchstone, New York, NY. 1998.

The Everything Personal Finance Book. Manage, Budget, Save and Invest Your Money Wisely! Peter Sander. Adams Media Corporation, Avon MA. 2003.

The Four Pillars of Investing. Lessons for Building a Winning Portfolio. William Bernstein. McGraw-Hill, New York NY. 2002.

Investment Philosophies. Successful Strategies and the Investors Who Made Them Work. Aswath Damodaran. John Wiley & Sons, Inc., Hoboken NJ. 2003.

Manias, Panics and Crashes. A History of Financial Crisis. Charles P. Kindleberger. John Wiley & Sons, Inc., New York NY. 2000.

The Millionaire Next Door. The Surprising Secrets of America's Wealthy. Thomas J. Stanley and William D. Danko. Pocket Books. New York NY. 1996.

Naked Economics. Undressing the Dismal Science. Charles Wheelan. W.W. Norton & Company, Inc. New York NY. 2002.

The New Life Insurance Investment Advisor. Ben C. Baldwin. Probus Publishing Company. Chicago IL. 2001.

The Overspent American. Why We Want What We Don't Need. Juliet B. Schor. Basic Books. New York NY. 1998.

The Prudent Investor's Guide to Beating Wall Street at its Own Game. John J. Bowen Jr & Daniel C. Goldie. McGraw-Hill, New York NY. 1998.

A Random Walk Down Wall Street. The Best Investment Advice for the New Century. Burton G. Malkiel. W.W Norton & Company. New York NY. 1999.

The Successful Investor Today. 14 Simple Truths You Must Know When You Invest. Larry E. Swedroe. St Martin's Press, New York NY. 2003.

Sudden Money. Managing a Financial Windfall. Susan Bradley with Mary Martin. John Wiley & Sons, Inc., New York NY. 2000.

Toward Rational Exuberance. The Evolution of the Modern Stock Market. B. Mark Smith. Farrar, Straus and Giroux. New York NY. 2001.

What's the Economy Trying to Tell You? Everyone's Guide to Understanding and Profiting From the Economy. David M. Blitzer. McGraw-Hill, New York NY. 1997.

APPENDIX F

Sustainable Withdrawal-Rate: Research Sources

This article summary is from the website www.journalfp.net (which is also www.fpanet.org/journal/) through the online tab called Past Issues and Articles where an extensive archive of articles resides from the *Journal of Financial Planning—The Official Publication of the Financial Planning Association.*

I provide this summary in a consolidated list for convenience to the reader, so you do not have to search through the main body of text to find references to these key concepts, ideas, and results. This approach, in itself, is different from the usual placement of references buried within the pages of the work. The philosophy in this method of presentation simplifies your ability to continue to follow the subject matter. You do not have to remember where in the text something was discussed. The use of the text is to make the point; the use of reference materials is to continue your own study into the subject matter. As I have said before, the role of a teacher is to teach you how to continue your own development of the ideas and concepts that you have initially been exposed to. A teacher cannot teach you everything, but can only point you in a direction so you continue to learn and develop the ideas for own use.

This material is the background material that I have used through my own research to develop the Wealth Rule and other principles presented in this work. I have presented the material in this work in a fashion that is different from what you may have seen before so you can take what used to be foggy concepts and turn them into something concrete (SOIL, WORM, Wealth Rule, Progress Line) that can be used to answer your most important questions as presented in the work.

Portfolio management and the sustainable withdrawal rate is an area that continues to be studied and subsequently refined by new research and findings. You should continue to follow this area as it develops, or ensure that your credentialed advisor is also.

This appendix provides background material that focuses on retirement issues. Appendix E provides the background material I used to integrated many other financial planning topics into the development of the WORM and the philosophy that supports an asset-based perspective as presented in this work.

1994 October Issue—Article 9
Determining Withdrawal Rates Using Historical Date
by William P. Bengen

1995 December Issue—Article 8
Playing the Averages: Estimating Retirement Income
by Michael D. Everett

1995 January Issue—Article 12
Plight of the Retiree: Inflation Versus Risk Aversion
by Keith V. Smith

1996 August Issue
Focus: The Changing Dynamics of Retirement

1997 February Issue—Article 12
Monitoring Retirement Portfolio Sufficiency
by Patrick J. Collins, Ph.D., CLU, PFP, Kristor J. Lawson, CFP, and Jon C. Chambers

1998 June Issue—Article 14
How Much Is Enough? A Guide to Planning for a Retirement Portfolio
by James K. Kennedy, Ph.D., Robert T. Nash, Ph.D., and John Andrew Bonno, Ph.D.

1998 December Issue
Focus: Managing Retirement Expectations

1999 February Issue—Article 9
Do Accumulation Models Over-state What's Needed to Retire?
by Kenn Tacchino, J.D., LL.M., RFP, and Cynthia Saltzman,Ph.D.

1999 May Issue—Article 5
The Catch-22 of Retirement
by Michael K. Stein, CFP

1999 June Issue—Article 12
Contributions: Sustainable Real Spending from Pensions and Investments
by Gordon Pye

1999 September Issue—Article 6
Checking the Expiration Date on Your Retirement Planning
by Michael K. Stein, CFP
Contributions: Sustainable Real Spending from Pensions and Investments

1999 September Issue—Article 13
Retirement Planning in the 21st Century
by William L. Anthes, Ph.D., and Bruce W. Most

2000 January Issue—Article 7
Meeting the Needs of Retirees: A Different Twist on Asset Allocation
by John Rekenthaler, CFA

2000 January Issue—Article 11
Optimum Withdrawals from an Asset Pool

2000 April Issue—Article 1
Retirement Mind Games
by Nancy Opiela

2000 April Issue—Article 2
The Four Percent Solution? Should financial planners ignore some old rules of
thumb when helping clients plan and manage their retirement?
by Shelley A. Lee

2000 July Issue—Article 3
Sustainable Retirement Spending For a Couple
by Gordon B. Pye, Ph.D.

2001 March Issue—Article 11
Should Social Security Be Included When Projecting Retirement Income?
by Kenn B. Tacchino, J.D., LL.M., RFC, and Cynthia Saltzman, Ph.D.

2001 April Issue—Article 13
Adjusting Withdrawal Rates For Taxes and Expenses
by Gordon B. Pye, Ph.D.

2001 July Issue—Article 1
Social Security Benefit Considerations in Early Retirement
by Clarence C. Rose, Ph.D., and L. Keith Larimore, Ph.D.

2001 December Issue—Article 6
Making Retirement Income Last a Lifetime
by John Ameriks, Ph.D., Robert Veres and Mark J. Warshawsky, Ph.D.

2002 April Issue—Article 9
Projecting Retirement Income by Running Portfolios over Historical Periods
by Michael D. Everett, Ph.D., and Murray S. Anthony, Ph.D., CPA

2003 May Issue—Article 9
Contributions: The Relation Between Portfolio Composition and Sustainable Withdrawal Rates
by Rory Terry

2004 January Issue—Article 10
Contributions—Does International Diversification Increase the Sustainable Withdrawal Rates from Retirement Portfolios?
by Philip I. Cooley, Ph.D.; Carl M. Hubbard, Ph.D.; Daniel T. Walz, Ph.D.

2004 February Issue
Focus: Distributions in Retirement

2004 February Issue—Article 1
Focus: Retirement Distributions: Creating a Limitless Income Stream for an 'Unknowable Longevity'
by Nancy Opiela

2004 March Issue—Article 8
The Best of 25 Years: Determining Withdrawal Rates Using Historical Data
by William Bengen

2004 July Issue—Article 7
Contribution: Sustainable Retirement Withdrawals
by Ahmet Tezel

Author Biography

Larry R. Frank Sr., MBA, CFP®

Larry was born in Duluth MN, and grew up in Cloquet MN. He has a B.S. Cum Laude in Physics (how things work) from the University of Minnesota. He also holds a Master's Degree in Business Administration (MBA) (how money works) from the University of South Dakota with a concentration in corporate finance and investments. He is a Certified Financial Planner™ practitioner (CFP®) with practical experience working with adults to address multiple financial topics simultaneously. He retired from the Air Force as a military officer in 1994 after a career as a helicopter and jet pilot, flying internationally in multiengine aircraft in 47 countries on five continents. He was also a contingency and war planner during the latter half of his career. This planning experience showed him how to think ahead and plan for alternative possibilities, important characteristics in any planning, including financial planning. In 1996, Larry founded Better Financial Education in Roseville CA, where the business focus is to teach and help people make smart decisions to grow and protect their net worth. He teaches local adult education classes in personal finance. He is a past director on the Board of Directors for the Financial Planning Association of Northern California. His hobbies include reading and travel, especially to an oceanfront home in El Salvador. He is married to Rosa Maria Cáceres from San Salvador, El Salvador, and currently lives in Rocklin CA. They have four children and two grandchildren.

0-595-33720-1

Printed in the United States
47525LVS00005B/141